STEFAN GATES

INCREDIBLE EDIBLES

WALKER BOOKS

AND SUBSIDIARIES

LONDON • BOSTON • SYDNEY • AUCKLAND

HELLO

I want to blow your mind. With food.

You see, I eat everything. I've had yak's penis and bull's bottom, rotten walrus and sheep's eyeballs, radioactive soup and bugs so big that you can see the "You're not really going to eat me?" look on their faces. But I don't eat to shock. I eat because I'm fascinated by the ideas hidden in our food: the fun, the science, the love, farts, disgust, laughter and adventure.

But the biggest adventures are with everyday ingredients: monster lollies and explosive flour, bee vomit and bug blood, eggs fried on paper, fish steamed in a dishwasher. When you look closely, everything edible hides something incredible.

Let's rip up the rules and manners that people have built around our meals – the ones that make food tidy, polite and good for you. Because if you do food right it shouldn't be good. It should be wild. It should be mind-blowing. And occasionally it should be just a leeeeeetle bit explosive!

There is another reason for eating everything on earth: because who knows what we might discover? The new potato? That insects burgers are better than beef? Something tastier than chocolate? Perhaps a whole new crop that could feed a hungry planet?

Take a deep breath, leave your fears and your hang-ups by the door and come with me. We're going on an adventure.

MAD RECIPES

Bring it ON! This is how food should be: fun, messy, rude and a bit crazy. Everything here is edible and delicious but the recipes might make you crease up with laughter, or fart your pants off.

CRAZY

Ever wondered how to eat a video camera, milk a camel or build a fart? The stories lurking behind our food are often bizarre and shocking. That's why I love them!

WEIRD FOOD

I've scoured the planet eating the weirdest, the slimiest and, frankly, the most terrifying foods on the planet. And here they are.

ABOUT THIS BOOK

How do you make a bum sandwich? Can you power a rocket with food? What's the most dangerous food on earth? Would you eat deep-fried scorpion? Packed full of mad recipes to cook for your friends, kitchen science projects to try out at home and completely bonkers food facts, this book will take you on a food adventure from breakfast right through to supper.

EXPERIMENTS

Careful, now. When you explore the science behind your food, you can discover some extraordinary, explosive, experimental secrets. But be warned – none of this is for eating.

STORIES

GASTROTRUMPS

CONTENTS

MAD RECIPES

WFS = Weird Food Story

CRAZY EXPERIMENTS

ADULT NEEDED

WHEREVER YOU SEE THIS SIGN YOU MAY NEED HELP
FROM AN ADULT. IT MIGHT BE FOR SOMETHING SIMPLE
LIKE CHOPPING, BLENDING, OR WHEN SOMETHING
GETS REALLY HOT. IT MIGHT MEAN THAT YOU NEED
SPECIALIST TOOLS OR AN ADULT WHO HAS DIY SKILLS.

MAD

RECIPES

ADULT NEEDED

KIT

A useful adult
Sieve
2 mixing bowls
Fork or potato masher

INGREDIENTS

2 cans of baked beans
Slice of buttered toast

HOW TO MAKE A GIANT BAKED BEAN

Beans, beans, good for your heart. The more you eat them, the more you get annoyed about how small they are and think how cool it would be to make a MASSIVE one. I tried to come up with some meaningful, educational reason for doing this, but I've given up. It's simple – why would you NOT make a giant baked bean? Especially handy if you have a hungry giant living with you.

METHOD

1. Open both cans and tip the baked beans into a small saucepan. With an adult to help you, warm them over a low heat, for 2 minutes only, stirring all the time. (Don't let them get too hot because you're going to have to handle them.)

2. Place a sieve over a bowl and pour your warm baked beans into it. Wait for 10 minutes for all of the tomato sauce to drain into the bowl leaving behind the naked baked beans. (Don't throw the sauce away – pour it back into the saucepan and keep warm – you'll need it later.) If there's still a lot of tomato juice on the beans, give them a stir with a wooden spoon, but try not to squish any beanage through the sieve.

3. Put the dry naked beans into a bowl and squish them with a fork or potato masher until thoroughly mashed into a pulp. Test that the beans are cool enough to handle then grab them with your hands and mould them into one massive bean shape.

4. Put the bean on a slice of hot buttered toast, pour over the warm tomato sauce and serve it to any giant you happen to have knocking around the house.

LAMB'S TESTICLES

THE STATS

From: Afghanistan
Taste: Deliciously, sweetly
meaty   **9/10**
Smell: Musky and offally   **5/10**
Texture: Amazingly
tender   **9/10**
Looks: Veiny egg   **2/10**
Adventure level:
Lip-curler   **9/10**
Nutrition:
Great protein and fat   **8/10**
£ Value: **Cheap as chips**

THE LOWDOWN

Yowch. If you're going to eat meat, an animal is going to die for your supper so you should be prepared to do the decent thing and throw as little of it away as possible ... which means eating all its bits and bobs. These can be grilled or BBQ'd and they're available in the UK from Turkish and Pakistani butchers. They call these "Lamb Eggs", which is odd, if you think about it.

ADULT NEEDED

KIT

An adult
Bucket of water to dunk the
"frying pan" into in case
of flames
Wet tea towel or fire extinguisher
(if you have one) to smother
potential flames
Wire coat-hanger
Pair of pliers
4 bulldog clips
Piece of plain white
or brown paper
The smallest gas burner on your
hob or small camping stove

INGREDIENTS

Splash of vegetable oil
1 egg at room temperature

HOW TO FRY AN EGG ON A PIECE OF PAPER

Yup, you really can fry an egg on a piece of paper. You probably won't believe this until you see it, but before you go burning the house down, let's just calm down a bit and think about why it might work.

Why? Well, the water in the egg soaks through the paper, allowing it to conduct heat through itself and into the egg. The paper will *eventually* burn, but only a long time after the egg has been burned to a cinder. If a flame touches bare paper it will burn, so the trick is to only let the flame heat the part of paper that is topped by egg. The easiest way to do this is to use a small, compact flame. That way, the egg will cook before it begins to burn. If possible, do this outside on a small camping stove. It will work indoors, but be careful! Wherever you do it, make sure you always have an adult on hand.

METHOD

1. Fill a bucket or sink with water, ready to douse any flames. This is non-negotiable – you MUST have this as there's a real chance you'll need it. If you've got a fire extinguisher have that standing by too.
2. Using a pair of pliers, pull the long straight length of the coat-hanger away from the hook and twist it around until the whole thing resembles an 8 cm x 8 cm square with a handle at each end (see pictures). Mould it so that it sits flat on the table.
3. Lay this "frying pan" frame on top of your piece of paper and cut around it to give you a piece with a 2 cm border all round. Fold the edges over the wire and hold them in place using bulldog clips

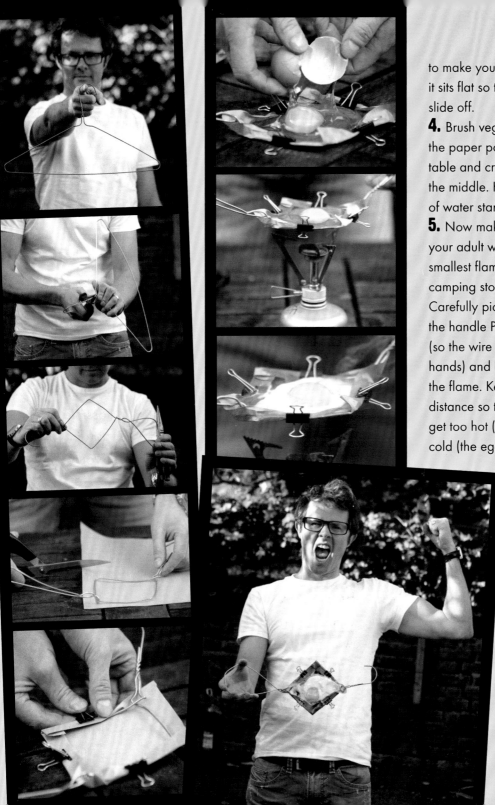

to make your pan. Check that it sits flat so that the egg won't slide off.

4. Brush vegetable oil all over the paper pan. Put it flat on the table and crack the egg into the middle. Have your bucket of water standing by.

5. Now make sure you have your adult with you. Turn on the smallest flame of your hob or camping stove and keep it low. Carefully pick the pan up using the handle PLUS a pair of pliers (so the wire doesn't burn your hands) and hold the pan over the flame. Keep adjusting the distance so that the pan doesn't get too hot (it will burn) or too cold (the egg won't cook). If it starts to smoke, lift it away from the flame for a few seconds. After about 1 minute, the egg will start to cook, turning white. After 5 minutes or so it will be cooked through.

6. Now it's ready to eat!

Eggshells
Paint or coloured pens and
  scraps of paper
Glue
Cotton wool
Cress seeds
Eggcups

MICROFACT

DOES CHEESE MAKE YOU DREAM?
SOMETIMES. IF YOU HAVE VIVID
DREAMS AFTER EATING CHEESE IT'S
PROBABLY DOWN TO YOUR SLEEP
PATTERNS BEING DISRUPTED BY ALL
THE HARD WORK YOUR DIGESTIVE
SYSTEM IS DOING.

EGGHEADS

Punk food! Oh, yeah!

After you've eaten your boiled eggs, don't chuck those poor, innocent eggshells into the compost – give them a second life. These cress eggheads are dead easy to make because cress grows so fast and makes a brilliant head of alien hair. It does take a few days to germinate but it's fun stuff. It also tastes cool – although it's related to the cabbage, it tastes slightly oniony, with the pepperiness of rocket salad. Its wonderful pungent flavour comes from compounds called aldehydes, including one that's found in almonds: benzaldehyde.

METHOD

1. Eat a nice boiled egg for breakfast and be careful not to damage the shell. Dig out every remaining bit of egg and give it a quick rinse with water.

2. Paint on the face of a loved one (or mortal enemy) as you see fit. I cut out eyes and lips but you could use a picture if you like.

3. Grab a small handful of cotton wool and soak it in water. Gently stuff it into the eggshell so that it's about half full.

4. Sprinkle a layer of cress seeds onto the wet cotton wool.

5. Cover the eggshell with a bit of paper for the first few days so that the seeds are in the dark when they start to germinate (that means when the seeds start to grow).

6. After a couple of days, when you see the seeds sprouting, take the paper off and move the egg to a bright place next to a window.

7. Sprinkle with a few drops of water every day to keep the cotton wool damp.

8. After a week or so your egg should have a healthy head of hair. Harvest your crop when it's about 8 cm high and eat it in a sandwich. Then, change the cotton wool and start again.

THE STATS

From: Mexico
Taste: Salty — 2/10
Smell: Swampy — 2/10
Texture: They crunch on the tongue — 7/10
Looks: Creamy sand — 5/10
Adventure level: Deeply unsettling but oddly quite easy to scoff — 8/10
Nutritional value: Loads of protein — 8/10
£ Value: Big treat

THE LOWDOWN

An ancient Mayan delicacy collected from a lake outside Mexico City and dried out. They are mixed into little patties with eggs and thinly sliced cactus leaf. They aren't really eaten for their taste but for their lightly crunchy texture.

KIT

1 clean jam jar with lid
Sieve
Clean tea towel
Big bowl
A friend to help with jam jar shaking

INGREDIENTS

200 ml fresh double cream
(a small pot)

WHAT'S REALLY HAPPENING

Milk, cream and butter are all basically the same substance but with different proportions of butter fat and whey (a watery liquid). Butter fat floats in tiny microscopic globules. In raw milk, a lot of butter fat floats to the top and can be scooped off as cream. When you shake this cream, the fat globules stick together, and you can drain off the whey to leave butter behind.

MICROFACT

THE MILK MOST OF US DRINK IS DIFFERENT TO RAW MILK. IT'S BEEN PASTEURIZED (HEATED TO 71.7°C TO KILL MOST OF THE BACTERIA IN IT) AND HOMOGENIZED (SPRAYED THROUGH A NOZZLE TO BREAK UP THE CREAMY BUTTER FAT INTO TINY DROPLETS THAT DON'T STICK TOGETHER).

DIY BUTTER

Back in the olden days when your mum, dad and other dinosaurs roamed the earth, people made their own butter. Or at least people who lived near a friendly cow did.

My mum used to spend hours in the morning making it from the creamy top part of fresh milk (the cream floats to the top), but these days we can buy double cream so half the work is already done for you. It only takes a few minutes and it's pretty cool, too.

METHOD

1. Take the cream out of the fridge 20 minutes before starting. (You don't have to, but this makes it a lot quicker.)

2. Pour the cream into the jam jar until it's half full and screw the lid on really tightly.

3. Shake the jam jar really hard for ... well ... as long as it takes. Sometimes 3 minutes, sometimes 15 minutes. It can be hard work, so get a friend to help. Keep going until you can feel a bit of a "thud" inside the jar as you shake.

4. Take a look in the jar. When it's ready there'll be a ball of butter sitting in a pool of what looks like watery milk (this is "whey").

5. Put the sieve over the bowl and lay the tea towel on top of it. Pour in everything from the jar. The whey will soak through and the butter will be left on top.

6. Lift up the corners of the tea towel with one hand and turn the butter in the middle to squeeze out all the water. If you fancy salted butter you can mix in ½ a teaspoon of fine salt.

7. Unwrap the butter and spread it onto hot toast.

8. Any left-over butter can be kept in the fridge for up to 10 days.

HOW MARGARINE WAS INVENTED

Ever eaten cow's udder? Most people haven't but it was used to make the first margarine, a cheap butter substitute invented by French scientist Hippolyte Mège-Mouriès in 1869. Why? Well, the Emperor of France, Napoleon III (who was a bit less warmongering than the great Napoleon I but a bit more warmongering than Napoleon II) was desperate to do a bit more warmongering. His armies needed high-fat food to keep them fighting a long way from home. Butter was just too expensive, so he set up a competition offering a prize to anyone who could invent a way of turning vegetable oil into a solid butter-like fat.

That same year Mège-Mouriès came up with the idea of using a bit of cow's udder and churning it with milk to try and get it to set into a solid. He thought that it would work in the same

way that rennet (an enzyme-rich substance from calves' stomachs) is used to turn milk into solid cheese. It was a good idea, but it didn't actually work very well.

Eventually he managed to mix a substance made from cheap beef tallow (fat from around the loins and kidneys of a cow which stays edible for ages without needing to be kept in a fridge), together with skimmed milk (which has lots of milk protein but is also dead cheap). Bingo: margarine, old-style.

These days spreads are usually made by mixing skimmed milk and vegetable oils with the help of chemicals known as emulsifiers. It's all heated and mixed before cooling into a spreadable solid. I know all of this because I have a huge book called *Margarine: An Economic, Social and Scientific History, 1869–1969* and I've actually read it. I am a bit weird.

HOW TO MILK A CAMEL

When I was travelling in Israel, I met a camel owned by a Bedouin herdsman who suggested that I'd like to milk her. She wasn't quite as enthusiastic as he was, but I thought I'd have a go anyway. Here's how you go about it: approach with caution, speaking in a soft voice and trying not to make

MICROFACT

CAN YOU MILK A CAT? YOU CAN, BUT YOU SHOULDN'T. A CAT'S KITTENS NEED ALL THE MILK SHE PRODUCES. YOU CAN BUY "CAT MILK" FOR KITTENS THAT AREN'T GETTING ENOUGH FROM THEIR MOTHER, BUT IT'S USUALLY COW'S MILK THAT'S BEEN PROCESSED TO MAKE IT SAFE FOR KITTENS TO DRINK.

any sudden moves that might frighten the lady. Take one of her teats in your hand and hold it at the top. It's a little like getting the last bit of toothpaste out of a tube: you have to trap the milk in the lower bit of the teat, and then squeeze the whole thing to squirt it out.

At this point, the camel will try to knock your block off. (Quite rightly, I may add. I mean this is intimate stuff, and camels don't take too kindly to strangers.) She will kick out at you with a mean strike, while all your new friends laugh at you and refuse to help. Persevere, but try to keep your legs out of range

(that's what I'm doing in the photo). Hold the cup or bucket under the teat and carry on squeezing, letting the teat refill between each squeeze. When you've got all you need, say thank you and retreat. Drink. It's heavy, warm but delicious stuff.

ME MILKING A CAMEL

GASTROTRUMPS
CAMEL HUMP

THE STATS
From: China
Taste: Luncheon meat — 6/10
Smell: Dog food — 3/10
Texture: Soft and slimy — 2/10
Looks: Hot dog meat — 3/10
Adventure level: Odd, but not that odd — 7/10
Nutritional value: High fat and protein — 6/10
£ Value: Wallet-buster

THE LOWDOWN
Camel meat is lean and can be tough, but hump is the opposite: soft and fatty, like cow's udder. It sounds fun to order in restaurants, but it's disappointingly dull to eat.

INGREDIENTS

Punnet of raspberries
Packet of sugar-coated chocolates
   or small round sweets

MICROFACT

RASPBERRIES CAN BE WHITE,
ORANGE AND PURPLE AS WELL AS
THE TRADITIONAL RED. THEY WERE
MENTIONED BY A BONKERS ROMAN
FELLA CALLED PLINY THE ELDER
2000 YEARS AGO. HE RECKONED
YOU COULD CURE A SCORPION BITE
BY POPPING THE ASHES OF A
RASPBERRY INTO A GLASS OF
WINE AND DRINKING IT.

CHOCOLATE-INJECTED FRUIT

Grown-ups want you to eat fruit. You want to eat chocolate. Stop fighting and combine the fruit with the chocolate! If you're really sneaky, you could probably make the grown-ups think that you're eating fruit when you're actually eating chocolate. Get IN!

METHOD

1. Put chocolates into raspberries. Erm ... that's it, really.

BEE VOMIT

THE STATS

From: All over the world

Taste: Sweet, very sweet 10/10

Smell: Flowery, treacly 8/10

Texture: Very, very sticky 9/10

Looks: Solid wee 1/10

Adventure level: Bee vomit has to be the world's weirdest food! 10/10

Nutritional value: Packed with energy 9/10

£ Value: Pocket money

THE LOWDOWN

It's the most disgusting-sounding food on earth – honey. As bees visit plants, they swallow a tiny bit of the sweet nectar from inside the flowers. Then, as they fly home the nectar starts to break down into sugars called sucrose and fructose. When the bees get back to the hive, they vomit the broken down nectar. Then their mates eat it and re-vomit it all over again. Between millions of visits, we get enough honey to spread on our toast. Enjoy!

ADULT NEEDED

MAKES: 5 litres of concentrate

KIT

A grown-up
Big, very clean bucket
Big saucepan
2 clean tea towels
Sieve
Enough bottles to store 5 litres
   of cordial

INGREDIENTS

2 carrier bags crammed full of
   fresh elderflower heads (about
   50)
4 lemons, juiced (keep the skins)
3 litres water
200 g citric acid or ascorbic acid
   (vitamin C powder)
3.5 kg sugar

LIQUID SUNSHINE ELDERFLOWER CORDIAL

This is an amazingly refreshing summer drink, especially when mixed with a bit of fizzy water – and the main ingredient is FREE! Elderflowers come out at the start of summer. The flowers are tiny, delicate little white things attached to spindly green twigs – check with your adult before you pick any. You also need citric or ascorbic acid, which you can get from chemists, or online.

METHOD

1. Spread your elderflowers out on the kitchen surface and throw away any that are covered in greenfly.

2. Put the flowers into the clean bucket along with the lemon juice, lemon skins and citric or ascorbic acid.

3. With an adult to help you, boil 3 litres of water, let it cool for 5 minutes and pour it over the elderflowers. Stir carefully.

4. Cover the bucket with a tea towel and leave it somewhere cool and undisturbed for 3 days, stirring it thoroughly every day.

5. Lay a sieve over your big saucepan and put a clean tea towel over it. Get someone to hold it in place, then slowly pour the flower water into the saucepan. You want just the flavoured water in the saucepan and all the twigs, flowers and bugs in the tea towel. Throw the contents of the tea towel away and put it in the wash.

6. Add the sugar to the pan and get an adult to help you put it on a medium heat. Heat it and stir until all of the sugar has dissolved, then turn the heat off and leave it for 30 minutes or so to cool down.

7. Pour the cordial into clean bottles and store them in the fridge.

8. To mix up your drink use about ⅕ cordial to ⅘ water.

PORCUPINE STEW

THE STATS

From: Cameroon

Taste: Diesel fuel	1/10
Smell: Meaty	2/10
Texture: Bony and fatty	2/10
Looks: Chicken stew	6/10
Adventure level: Spiky, but not very tasty	5/10
Nutritional value: Good balanced meal	9/10
£ Value:	**Pocket money**

THE LOWDOWN

Porcupine meat is very popular in Cameroon. To prepare it, the porcupine is dunked in boiling water and all the spines are pulled out. Then the meat is chopped and boiled with vegetables. It tastes rank. Although porcupines aren't endangered, there's a fair amount of evidence that the trade in wild animal meat (bushmeat) is harming biodiversity.

ADULT NEEDED

MAKES: 1 bottle of concentrate

KIT

A well-behaved adult
Grater
Large saucepan
Sieve
Large bowl
Clean tea towel
Clean bottle

INGREDIENTS

2 oranges
2 limes
1 lemon
1 tbsp fresh ginger, grated
4 drops vanilla flavouring
1 tsp ascorbic acid (vitamin C powder – you can buy it at the chemist)
Large pinch ground nutmeg
Large pinch ground cinnamon
Large pinch ground star anise (you may need to grind this yourself in a pestle and mortar)
1 tsp caramel colouring (optional)
200 ml water
450 g caster sugar
50 g dark brown muscovado sugar

HOW TO MAKE YOUR OWN COLA

I'll be honest with you – this doesn't taste *exactly* the same as the leading brands of cola. It tastes like a home-made version of them. To make the real stuff you need all sorts of gubbins like food-grade essential oils (which are really expensive), pure caffeine, kola nuts and citric acid. I made it on TV once and it was fun, but very tricky. This recipe is much easier, although you do need to go shopping for a few ingredients before you start. If there's any ingredient that you can't find, don't worry too much – as long as you've got most of them you'll probably still make a fantastic drink.

METHOD

1. Grate the zest (the outside skin) of the oranges, lemons and limes and put it in a saucepan. Squeeze the lemon, lime and orange juice into the saucepan, and throw away the leftovers.

2. Put all the other ingredients except the sugars into the saucepan, add 200 ml of water, put a lid on and with an adult to help you, simmer it on a very gentle heat for 20 minutes. Add the sugars and stir until dissolved.

3. Put the sieve on the large bowl, lay the tea towel over it and pour the liquid through. Throw away the mucky bits and put the tea towel in the laundry bin. The sugary liquid is your syrup. Keep it in a clean bottle in the fridge.

4. To make a glass of cola, pour 60 ml of your syrup into a glass and add 200 ml fizzy water.

MICROFACT

EVERYTHING IS TOXIC IF YOU EAT TOO MUCH TOO QUICKLY — EVEN APPLES AND CABBAGE COULD KILL. THE BASIC PRINCIPLE OF TOXICOLOGY IS THAT IT'S NOT THE SUBSTANCE THAT'S DANGEROUS BUT THE AMOUNT OF IT YOU EAT.

ROASTED GRASSHOPPERS
(OR CHAPPULINES)

THE STATS
From: Mexico

Taste: Nicely sour		9/10
Smell: Musty		3/10
Texture: Crunchy		9/10
Looks: Grasshopper-like		8/10
Adventure level: Think of them as crisps		8/10
Nutritional value: Loads of protein, low-fat		10/10
£ Value:		Pocket money

THE LOWDOWN
Roasted grasshoppers are hugely popular in warmer parts of the world as they are easy and cheap to collect or farm, and they reproduce incredibly quickly. These ones are roasted with lime and chilli to make a great tangy snack.

ADULT NEEDED

KIT

A grown-up
2 or 3 terracotta flowerpots about
  12 – 15 cm diameter at the top –
  new and thoroughly clean
Large mixing bowl
Clingfilm

INGREDIENTS

500 g strong white bread flour
  plus a bit extra for dusting
  (or 350 g white flour and 150 g
  wholemeal flour)
2 tsp salt
1 x 7 g sachet of fast-action
  dried yeast
3 tbsp olive oil or vegetable oil
300 ml water
50 g butter

FLOWERPOT BREAD

Some household objects are useful for cooking and some are not. Spades are great for frying eggs over bonfires, metal bins make wicked pizza ovens and dishwashers are ace for cooking salmon in. Tumble-dryers, however, are totally rubbish for making scrambled eggs. I know this because I tried and failed. Spectacularly and expensively.

  Flowerpots are great for baking bread in. And cakes, too. They've been fired in a kiln, so they should be able to withstand the kind of heat it takes to bake stuff.

METHOD

1. Clean your flowerpots thoroughly.
2. In the large mixing bowl, mix together the flour, salt and yeast. Make a little well in the middle and pour the oil and water into it. Mix well, using a wooden spoon or your hands, until it turns into dough.
3. Spread a small handful of flour over a clean kitchen surface and tip the dough onto it. Now knead it. (This is basically beating it up for a while so that you change its microscopic structure and make it more elastic. It's hard work, but fun.) Push down and away from you hard with the heel of your palm to squish the dough, then fold it back onto itself, spin it 90 degrees and push again. Keep doing this for about 5 – 10 minutes until the dough feels smooth and tight.
4. Using a piece of kitchen roll, spread a little vegetable oil all over the inside of your mixing bowl. Put the dough into the bowl and cover with a piece of clingfilm. Place this somewhere warm for an hour and it should double in size.
5. If your flowerpots have holes in the bottom, put a small piece of foil over the holes. Grease the insides and bottom of the pots with lots of butter – use a piece of kitchen roll again – so that the cooked bread will come out easily. They should be *very* buttery.

6. Take the dough out of the bowl and "knock it back" by kneading it again for about 1 minute.

7. Divide the dough up between your flowerpots so that they're about ½ to ⅔ full. Scatter a dusting of flour over the top and then put them back into a warm place for an hour until they've doubled in size again.

8. At this point, you might need an adult to help you heat your oven to 220°C/gas 7 and put the flowerpots in to bake for 15–30 minutes depending on the size of your pots. Check them after 15 minutes. When cooked, they should have a nice brown crust and a slightly hollow sound when tapped with a wooden spoon.

9. Leave the flowerpots to cool for 10 minutes or so before serving.

ADULT NEEDED

MAKES: 6 portions (depending on the size of your loaf)

KIT
A sensible adult
Knife
Clingfilm

INGREDIENTS
1 loaf of good bread (NOT sliced)
Left-over pasta with Bolognese sauce
1 jar of roasted pepper antipasti

MICROFACT
DO CARROTS MAKE YOU SEE IN THE DARK? NO. THIS WAS A RUMOUR SPREAD DURING WWII BY THE BRITS, WHO WANTED TO KEEP THE INVENTION OF RADAR SECRET. THAT SAID, THE VITAMIN A FOUND IN CARROTS (AMONGST OTHER FOODS) IS GOOD FOR YOUR EYES.

MEAL-IN-A-LOAF

A brilliant dish for a picnic: lunch served in a whole loaf of bread. You just hollow a loaf out, fill it with food and pop the lid back on. You can carry it around until you want to eat. This isn't just a naughty, cheeky way of mucking about with your food. I mean, it IS naughty and cheeky, but it's also based on a classic dish from Provence, in the south of France, called a *pan bagnat*. So that's all right, then.

You can put pretty much any combination of food into the loaf – just don't use soggy ingredients or it'll disintegrate before you get around to eating it. The classic French version uses grilled vegetables, but you could try fish and chips or simply fill it with ham, cheese, tomatoes and salad.

METHOD
1. With an adult to help you, slice the top off your loaf, about ¼ of the way down, keeping it in one piece. Lift it off and put it aside.
2. Pull most of the soft bread innards out using your fingers, but leave a good 3 cm or so at the bottom. (Otherwise the whole thing will collapse!)
3. Put a layer of roasted peppers at the bottom of the loaf, then tip in a good amount of left-over pasta and Bolognese sauce. Pack it in firmly, then top with another layer of peppers.
4. Put the lid back on.
5. Wrap the whole thing in clingfilm and put it in the fridge with a weight on top. (Try a plate weighed down with cans of food.)
6. Leave it for a few hours to chill out.
7. To eat, unwrap it and cut into slices like a cake.

MAKES: 1 sandwich

KIT
Clingfilm

INGREDIENTS
2 slices bread
2 tbsp olive oil
Handful grated Cheddar cheese
Handful fresh basil leaves
Handful lettuce
1 tbsp grated Parmesan cheese
Salt and pepper

TOP TIP
This works with pretty much any sandwich but this cheese and basil mix is particularly tasty when it's been sat on.

BUM SANDWICH

When I meet the kids who are going to star in each new episode of my TV series they can be pretty nervous. It's not surprising: it is scary having four cameras and a hundred people staring at you just as you're about to do something bonkers with food! I like to get them a bit more relaxed by doing something fun and naughty like making a bum sandwich.

But sitting on a sandwich isn't just for giggles and sniggers. It's about using your body temperature (37.5°C) to warm the food up, because warm food has a deeper smell and taste than cold food. The warmer a substance is, the more active its tiny molecules are, and that goes for the molecules that make up flavours too. When they're warm they move around a lot more and zip up your nose so that you get a stronger

GASTROTRUMPS
SILK WORM PUPAE

THE STATS
From: South Korea
Taste: Mouldy, yet nutty   1/10
Smell: Mouldy   4/10
Texture: Soggy, chewy insect guts   2/10
Looks: Scary rabbit poo   1/10
Adventure level: This one's a *real* challenge   10/10
Nutrition: Some good protein   6/10
£ Value: **Pocket money**

THE LOWDOWN
These are eaten as a snack in many Asian countries. In South Korea these are called Beondegi and are usually boiled or steamed, which softens the hard casings of them a little. As you bite in, you find a mass of soft insect guts, but parts of the shells are almost impossible to chew, so you have to just swallow and hope for the best. Korean grocers sell them in cans.

experience of a food's flavour. Added to that, your body weight squishes the herbs in the sandwich, releasing the lovely flavour oils in them. Basically, your bum is used as a gentle cooker to make your sarnie taste better and your weight is used as a flavour press. Genius.

METHOD

1. Lay your bread out, pour a good pool of olive oil on each slice and spread it out to the edges. (In this sandwich I'm using oil instead of butter.)

2. Scatter the rest of the ingredients over one side of the sandwich, making sure they cover the slice of bread.

3. Put the sandwich together and press down on it to get rid of some of the air in the bread. Wrap it up in about 5–6 layers of clingfilm, tucking in the sides as you go.

4. Now sit on it for as long as you can wait. 10 minutes is fine but 30 minutes is great.

5. Cut it open with scissors and scoff.

INSECT EATING

We don't eat a lot of bugs in this country, but they're a really important food in many places around the world. I've eaten fantastic worms, flies and fat-bottomed ants in Mexico, massive weevils in Cameroon, maggots in Burma, silkworm pupae in South Korea and all manner of wriggly fun in Thailand.

Why? Well, insects are a brilliant way of turning vegetable matter into delicious protein. In the UK, most cows are fed on grain and it can take 20–50 kg of grain to produce 1 kg of beef. That's a huge amount of grain (as well as fertilizer and other resources needed to grow it) to take out of the food chain. It's a pretty inefficient way of using the planet's resources. Many people around the world go hungry, so although many of us love beef, we also need to think about the best way to use our food and land.

Solution? INSECTS! Many insects use less than 2 kg of vegetable matter to produce 1 kg of edible protein, they grow amazingly fast and reproduce very quickly (unlike cows) so it seems crazy not to eat them.

There's one hiccup – in the UK, most insects are calorie-neutral which means that you use up as many calories hunting them as you get from eating them because our climate isn't ideal for finding or farming insects. The best climate is often in

developing countries. So if they could sell us their bugs, they'd make some money, and we'd get delicious food.

It's best not to collect your own bugs in the UK – not many people know which are the safest insects to eat and, unless they've been farmed properly, they could have been crawling on unsafe things like weedkiller or dog poo!

One last thought on insect eating: people think that insects are eaten raw and wriggling because they've watched gruesome challenges on the telly. That's just silly. In my travels, I've almost NEVER eaten insects raw. They're usually roasted or dry-fried, because it brings out the flavour in them.

Go on, pack away your fears and give them a go.

PALM WEEVILS

MICROFACT

SWEETS ARE OFTEN MADE WITH BUGS' BLOOD. IF YOU SEE E120 OR "COCHINEAL" WRITTEN ON THE INGREDIENTS LIST, IT'S MADE USING PINK-PURPLE CRUSHED COCHINEAL BEETLES.

MBOO GRUBS

MAGUEY PLANT
WORM

GASTROTRUMPS
DEEP-FRIED SCORPIONS

THE STATS

From: China
Taste:
Fishy, sweet like prawns   **6/10**
Smell: None really   **0/10**
Texture: Crunchy, with a
soft centre   **7/10**
Looks:
Aargh! Like a SCORPION! **1/10**
Adventure level:
Scorpions kill, don't they? **10/10**
Nutritional value:
High protein   **7/10**
£ Value: **Big treat**

THE LOWDOWN

In China, scorpions are eaten
fried, grilled or roasted. Heat
makes their venom harmless, but
they are served live in specialist
restaurants. (With their stingers
cut off, thankfully.)

ADULT NEEDED

MAKES: 4 big portions of soup

KIT
An adult
Chopping board and knife
Big pan
Wooden spoon
Blender

INGREDIENTS
2 tbsp olive oil
4 cloves garlic, chopped
2 onions, chopped
1 pig's trotter (ask the butcher to
   split it in two if you can)
500 ml chicken or vegetable stock
   made up from stock cubes
700 g frozen peas
Salt and pepper

MICROFACT

IRRADIATED FOOD HAS BEEN EXPOSED
TO RADIATION, WHICH STERILIZES IT,
KILLING BACTERIA AND OTHER
MICRO-ORGANISMS. IT'S NOT
RADIOACTIVE, AND IT'S ACTUALLY
VERY USEFUL FOR SICK HOSPITAL
PATIENTS AND ASTRONAUTS.

SNOT AND FOOT SOUP

Some doctors say that eating bogies is good for you – the small amounts of bacteria in them boost your immune system, apparently. Sadly, it's almost impossible to collect enough bogies for a decent bowl of soup unless you've got a really vicious bout of the flu, in which case you probably won't feel like eating anyway.

Basically this is a big green pea soup, and there's no real snot in it. But it does taste lovely and rich if you can find a pig's foot to add to it – just leave it out if you can't.

METHOD

1. With an adult to help you, heat the oil in a big saucepan and add the garlic, onion and pig's trotter. Cook over a low heat for about 15 minutes, stirring every now and then until the onions go a bit see-through. Don't let them burn.

2. Add the stock, and bring to a very gentle boil. Simmer for 10 minutes.

3. Take the pan off the hob, add the peas, and return it to the heat and let it simmer for 2 more minutes. Then take it off the heat and allow the soup to cool slightly.

4. Take the trotter out and put it to one side while your adult helper blends the soup using a hand blender. Add salt and pepper to taste.

5. Pour the soup into bowls, putting the chunk of trotter in the bowl of your most easily scared friend.

ADULT NEEDED

SERVES: 2

KIT

A tame adult
Pliers
Piece of chicken wire or an old
  wire grill from a disposable BBQ
Gloves
Hammer and screwdriver
Empty chocolate tin (you know –
  those 1 kg tins)
Handful of hardwood sawdust
  or smoking chips (buy online or
  from fishing tackle shops)

INGREDIENTS

2 x 150 g skinless fillets of salmon
Vegetable oil
200 g cooked noodles (follow
  packet instructions)
Small handful coriander, chopped
2 tbsp soy sauce
Salt and pepper

MICROFACT

FUGU, THE TOXIC LIVER OF
PUFFERFISH, IS DEADLY BUT THE
JAPANESE LOVE EATING IT. FUGU
CHEFS HAVE TO GET A SPECIAL
LICENCE. THE DANGER IS
FUN, BUT IT'S ACTUALLY
RELATIVELY TASTELESS.

HOW TO COOK IN A CHOCOLATE TIN

Ever experienced the hell of Granny nicking the last chocolate in the tin at Christmas? Me too. And grannies always wear that innocent "I can't do anything wrong because I'm sooooooo old" look on their faces. Don't be fooled – those oldies know exactly what they're doing.

To cheer yourself up, tell Granny that you're going to cook her supper in the empty tin and she'd better eat it or she's going to bed with an empty tum. This cooking method sounds weird, but it's BRILLIANT. The damp smoke smoulders in the tin, and the fish cooks through a combination of steam convection and heat radiation.

This is ONLY to be tried with an ADULT helping you. It can make a fair bit of smoke, so it works best outside, but if you're inside, make sure you open the windows before you start cooking!

METHOD

1. First make a shelf in the chocolate tin for the fish to sit on. Get your tame adult to bend and shape the chicken wire or BBQ grill so that it would sit halfway up the tin. It doesn't need to be too neat. (See photo, right.) The wire can be sharp, so they should wear gloves.
2. Ask your grown-up to whack 4–5 holes in the tin lid using a hammer and screwdriver.
3. Scatter a small handful (about 25 g) of hardwood sawdust in the base of the tin.
4. Add two tablespoons of water (no more) and slosh it around so that the sawdust gets a bit soggy. Now add your wire shelf to the tin.

5. Put your salmon fillets on a chopping board and rub each with a tablespoon of vegetable oil, spreading it all over them with your hands. Now wash your hands.

6. Lay the salmon fillets on the wire shelf and put the lid on.

7. With an adult to help, put the whole tin onto the hob and turn the heat on to medium. It will start smoking after a minute or two. Let it cook for 5 minutes and then turn the heat off. DON'T TOUCH THE TIN as it'll be very hot. Leave it for 5 minutes to cool down.

8. While the salmon is cooling, cook your noodles according to the instructions on the packet, then toss them in two tablespoons of vegetable oil, coriander and soy sauce.

9. Get your adult to open the tin, making sure they're wearing oven gloves. Check that your salmon is cooked – it should be slightly browned on the outside, smoky and hot in the middle.

10. Share the noodles out between two bowls or plates and lay the smoked salmon on top. Tuck in.

ADULT NEEDED

MAKES: 4 kebabs

KIT
An understanding adult and
  their car
Chicken wire
Galvanized metal wire (easily
  found in DIY shops)
Pliers
4 x 20 cm wooden kebab sticks
Foil

INGREDIENTS
300 g salmon fillet
1 red pepper
1 green pepper
1 tbsp olive oil
1 tbsp chopped fresh coriander
  (optional)
½ lemon
Salt and pepper

CAR ENGINE KEBABS

Adults just don't get it sometimes, do they? They're always annoyed when kids do something out-of-the-ordinary with their food. Why would you cook kebabs on a car engine, they ask? There's only one answer to a question as dim as this: BECAUSE YOU CAN.

This is best done on a summer car journey that's so long and boring you need a bonkers picnic at the end of it. Before you get into big trouble, though, bear in mind that this baby needs expertise. Take the owner of the car with you to find a mechanic and ask them which bit of the car: a) gets really hot (it's usually the manifold), and b) doesn't move, so you can safely attach something to it for a long car journey.

You MUST do this with the help of the adult who owns the car. If your folks let you do this, you can tell them from me: they rock!

METHOD

1. Make the kebabs – cut the salmon and pepper into chunks about 2 cm x 2 cm and push them onto the kebab sticks, alternating pepper and salmon until you have four separate kebabs.

2. Lay each kebab on a piece of foil measuring 50 cm x 30 cm. Splash a little olive oil all over them. Scatter the coriander, add a squeeze of lemon juice and season with salt and pepper.

3. Now wrap the kebabs up firmly in the foil by folding the ends over so that no car fumes can get in. Make sure the kebabs are covered in two layers, but no more, otherwise the heat won't get to the fish.

4. With help from your grown-up, make a little cage out of the chicken wire: cut a 30 cm x 30 cm piece and fold it into two so that you have a flattish 30 cm x 15 cm cage. Tie up the short sides of it using the galvanized wire, leaving the long top open. Get your grown-up to attach this to the place on the engine that your mechanic recommended, using more metal wire. It must be absolutely rock solid so that it won't fall off.

5. Carefully put the kebabs into the wire cage, making sure that you don't rip the foil.

6. Drive! A good 30 miles in the summer should be enough to cook the fish, but it can take longer in winter as the cold air moves around the engine, slowing the cooking process down. The fish is cooked when it has turned opaque. Check that it isn't completely raw in the middle, and if it is ... get back on the road until it's cooked through!

ADULT NEEDED

SERVES: 6

KIT

An adult
Frying-pan
Knife
Saucepan
Food processor or blender

INGREDIENTS

2 tbsp olive oil
1 large onion, peeled and sliced
2 cloves garlic, peeled and sliced
1 litre vegetable stock
1 x 400g can chopped tomatoes
2 x 250 g packs of cooked
  beetroot, drained and chopped
1 tbsp sugar
3 small balls of mozzarella or
  6 tbsp thick crème fraîche
3 stoned black olives,
  sliced in half

MICROFACT

BLOOD IS USED IN MANY DISHES
FROM AROUND THE WORLD, INCLUDING
BRITISH BLACK PUDDING (BLOOD
SAUSAGES), BOUDIN NOIR (THE SAME,
BUT FRENCH), DRISHEEN (IRISH SHEEP
AND BEEF BLOOD SAUSAGES) AND
DINUAGAN (MEAT STEWED IN BLOOD
AND VINEGAR FROM THE PHILIPPINES).
IT'S DARN FINE STUFF, TOO.

BLOOD SOUP WITH EYEBALLS

You gotta love it: a sea of beetroot soup with a blob of mozzarella in the middle. The whole thing looks like a cyclops on a bad day. It's actually a very typical Ukrainian dish that I ate a lot when I visited the nuclear power station at Chernobyl.

And there's the added bonus that it'll turn your poo red. I like that in a soup.

METHOD

1. With an adult on stand-by, heat the oil in a frying pan, add the onions and fry them very slowly (about 15 minutes if you can bear to wait that long). When they are just starting to brown, add the garlic and let it fry for another 5 minutes.
2. Meanwhile heat the stock and chopped tomatoes in a saucepan until simmering, then turn off the heat and stir in the chopped beetroot, sugar and at the last minute the onions and garlic.
3. Get your adult to help you transfer the mix, a batch at a time, into a food processor and blend until smooth.
4. Pour into wide bowls (not too deep otherwise the "eyeball" won't stand out), add a ball of mozzarella or spoonful of crème fraîche to each as an eyeball, and top each with half an olive (as the pupil). Aaaaah.

GASTROTRUMPS
SHEEP'S BLOOD

THE STATS

From: Ethiopia

Taste: Milky and sweet — 9/10

Smell: Very slightly spicy — 5/10

Texture: Creamy — 7/10

Looks: Vivid red — 8/10

Adventure level: Guilt- and vom-inducing — 10/10

Nutritional value: Good for desperate times — 8/10

£ Value: Big treat

THE LOWDOWN

Either for ceremonies or in times of great need, Ethiopians make a little cut in the neck of a live sheep, cow or goat and drain a small amount of blood from it. Afterwards the sheep hops away, a bit confused but OK.

ADULT NEEDED

STINGING NETTLE SOUP

SERVES: 4

KIT

A well-behaved adult
Rubber gloves
Colander
2 saucepans
Blender or food processor

INGREDIENTS

1 large carrier-bag packed with
young nettles
20 g butter
2 tbsp olive oil
1 onion, chopped
1 large potato, chopped
500 ml vegetable stock
200 ml full-fat milk
Salt and pepper

Oooouch! Nettles sting because when you brush against them, their bizarre little hairs act like teeny tiny needles and inject irritants called formic acid and histamines into your skin. This acid is neutralized by cooking, so you can get your own back on them 'orrible swines by eating them! They make a lovely, grassy-tasting soup.

It's best to pick young nettles at the start of the spring or summer – before June, really. Any later and they get a bit bitter.

METHOD

1. Wearing your rubber gloves, pick through the nettles and throw away the stalks – you just want nice small tender leaves.
2. Rinse the leaves in water and put them (without any extra water) into a large saucepan. Get your well-behaved adult to help you put

the pan on a low heat and simmer the leaves very gently for 10 minutes.
3. Put the cooked nettles in the colander and squish with the back of a spoon to get rid of the water. Put them back in the pan with the butter and once coated put them to one side.
4. Put the olive oil in your pan and gently fry the onions and potatoes for 10 minutes on a low heat. Add the vegetable stock and milk and simmer gently for 7–8 minutes. Turn the heat off and add the cooked nettles, then ask your grown-up to help you blend the mix in a couple of batches until smooth. Add salt and pepper.
5. Serve with nice crusty bread.

JELLYFISH

THE STATS

From: China
Taste: Tasteless   1/10
Smell: Odourless   1/10
Texture: Crunchy
and slimy   9/10
Looks: Grey strips   2/10
Adventure level: Will
they sting?   7/10
Nutritional value:
Mostly water   1/10
£ Value: Pocket money

THE LOWDOWN

Although jellyfish are tasteless,
once dressed with soy sauce,
lime juice, sesame oil and
coriander they make a cracking
salad, simply because the texture
is so unusual. You can buy them
in Chinese or Thai grocers, in
either salted or "instant" varieties.

ADULT NEEDED

SERVES: 4

KIT
A house-trained adult
Peeler
Knife
Saucepans

INGREDIENTS
500 g raw beetroot
250 g small salad potatoes
2 x 250 g asparagus bundles

For the dressing:
75 ml olive oil
20 ml white wine vinegar
1 tsp honey
½ tsp mustard
Salt and pepper

MICROFACT
ASPARAGUS REALLY DOES MAKE YOUR
WEE SMELL. THE SMELLY SULPHUROUS
CHEMICALS CREATED WHEN WE
DIGEST ASPARAGUS MAKE EVERYONE'S
WEE SMELL FUNNY, BUT NOT
EVERYONE CAN SENSE IT. I QUITE LIKE
THE SMELL, BUT THEN I'M ODD.

HOW TO MAKE YOUR WEE SMELLY AND YOUR POO RED

Asparagus wee STINKS! And beetroot makes your poo red. It can even make your wee red, if you eat enough. It's a great way to give your family and friends a big surprise.

Many people seem to be scared of beetroots, partly because they are usually so flipping badly cooked. This asparagus, beetroot and potato salad is a brilliant combination.

METHOD

1. Preheat the oven to 180°C/gas 4. Getting your adult to help you, peel and slice the beetroot into rough chunks about 3 cm square, then place them in a roasting tray. Pour over a splash of olive oil and toss them around until they are fully coated in it. Place a piece of foil loosely over the top and put them into the oven for 20–25 minutes until tender.

2. Meanwhile, boil the potatoes in water for about 15 minutes or until just tender. Then drain, rinse in cold water (to stop them overcooking) and put them back in the empty saucepan. Pour over a slosh of olive oil and toss them around to get covered.

3. Chop the woody ends off the asparagus (not the pointy tip – that's the best bit!) and boil them for about 4 minutes until just tender. Rinse to cool, then slice each spear into three short pieces. Add them to the potatoes.

4. Mix all the dressing ingredients together in a jam jar (a cup would do), then shake (or stir) thoroughly to mix them together.

5. Add the cooked beetroot to the asparagus and potatoes, then pour over the dressing and mix it all together.

6. Serve and reap the rewards!

DUCK TONGUES

THE STATS

From: China
Taste: Meaty — 7/10
Smell: Ducky (richer than chicken) — 7/10
Texture: Bony, tiny chicken drumstick — 6/10
Looks: Tongue on a stick — 2/10
Adventure level: It's quite a leap! — 9/10
Nutritional value: Decent protein — 5/10
£ Value: Big treat

THE LOWDOWN

Each duck tongue comes with its own handy little bone that you hold to chew from. The taste is mildly duck-like, but like so many Chinese dishes this one is about the sauce it's cooked in and the fun of eating something unusual, while also making the best use of every last bit of the animal.

KIT
An airtight lunch box
Dishwasher

INGREDIENTS
Salmon fillet – as many as you
   want (you'll need about 150 g
   per person)
Olive oil
Salt and pepper

TOP TIP
To serve, cook some steamed
potatoes or noodles and
glazed carrots.

HOW TO COOK SALMON IN A DISHWASHER

This isn't a joke. Dishwashers really are excellent cooking tools, especially for foods that are best cooked very gently. Restaurants splash out thousands of pounds buying "water baths" which poach food at very gentle temperatures, but if you've got one of these bad boys in your kitchen and your parents will let you use it for cooking, you're laughing. Most dishwashers heat up to 65°C, which is perfect for making lovely moist poached salmon. If you're not particularly fond of eating fish, it's worth plucking up the courage to eat this

simply for the fun of it all. Make sure you ask first and do check in the instructions (or online) that your dishwasher gets up to at least 60°C. Always use excellent quality fresh salmon.

Grown-ups might argue that the dishwasher itself might be too dirty to cook with. To which you should reply, "Well we eat off the plates that come out of it, don't we? Blimey, don't you want me to have any fun, like, ever?"

METHOD

1. Rinse your salmon fillet in cold water then pat it dry with kitchen roll.

2. Pop it in your lunch box and pour a glug of olive oil onto it. Spread the olive oil all over the fish using clean fingers or a piece of kitchen roll. Sprinkle a little salt and pepper on top.

3. Place the box on the top drawer of your dishwasher, with NO detergent or dirty plates in the machine. Select the hottest, or most intensive setting, and turn the dishwasher on. Most dishwashers take about an hour to complete the cycle. Some run a cold rinse at the end so that the plates aren't too hot to touch – so don't worry too much if your salmon is cold on the outside.

4. When the dishwasher cycle is finished, carefully take the box out, open it and check that the salmon is cooked. It should be pale on the outside and a little darker inside.

MICROFACT

HEADCHEESE IS A KIND OF PÂTÉ MADE BY BOILING A PIG'S HEAD FOR 3 HOURS AND PULLING ALL THE SKIN, MEAT AND BOBBLY BITS OFF. SOUNDS WEIRD, BUT TASTES WICKED.

GASTROTRUMPS
SURSTRÖMMING
(OR FERMENTED HERRINGS)

THE STATS
From: Sweden
Taste: Salty vomit   1/10
Smell: Vomit, poo
and rotten fish   1/10
Texture: Rotten fish guts   1/10
Looks: Mashed old fish   1/10
Adventure level:
Requires extreme bravery   10/10
Nutritional value:
Who cares? It's awful!   1/10
£ Value: **Big treat**

THE LOWDOWN
Why, oh why, oh why? Surströmming is without question the most evil-smelling, foul-tasting food on earth. I have made several people (including gastronautically-inclined TV presenters), physically sick by feeding them this stuff. Its only redeeming feature is that it was developed as a way of preserving fish in times of need. But if you need this stuff, you might as well call it a day.

DURIAN FRUIT

Durian fruit is hugely popular in Indonesia, Thailand and Malaysia. Despite being eye-bleedingly expensive, it HONKS! It's hard to describe the smell – it's somewhere in between vomit and death, with a bit of boiled cabbage and stinky pants thrown in.

In fact, they smell so bad that when I was staying in a hotel in Thailand, they actually had signs next to the lift saying, "No durians" and a picture of one with a red cross through it.

These fruit are huge – about the size of two or three pineapples – and covered in a vicious skin made of tough spikes. To get at the fist-sized segments of fruit and their large seeds, you have to cut through their angry hide with a knife.

So why are they so popular?

Well they taste heavenly – a bit like fragrant, flowery custard. They are used in lots of South East Asian dishes, salads and even as a flavouring for crisps. You can often find them at Chinese and Thai grocers. If you find one, have a try. Just don't breathe in.

POPPING CANDY

It may surprise you to learn that popping candy, also known as Space Dust, Pop Rocks or Fizz Wiz, doesn't actually come from space. Who knew?

This is the stuff that fizzes, pops and crackles on your tongue as you eat it. It was patented by an American dude called William Mitchell waaaay back in 1956, but wasn't sold publicly for another nineteen years.

It's made by mixing together sugar, lactose, glucose and flavouring, then heating it to make liquid candy, then adding carbon dioxide. But crucially, this mixing and cooking is done under pressure, so that as the sugar candy cools, sets and hardens, it traps little bubbles of carbon dioxide inside, still under pressure.

When you put the candy on your tongue, the moisture in your saliva starts to dissolve it, releasing the little trapped, pressurized carbon dioxide bubbles, which then create the crackling sound.

GASTROTRUMPS
SNAKE SKINS

THE STATS
From: China
Taste: Salty — 3/10
Smell: Musty, old oil — 4/10
Texture: Oily and crispy — 4/10
Looks: Bits of handbag — 2/10
Adventure level: A bit odd — 6/10
Nutritional value: Same as crisps — 2/10
£ Value: Big treat

THE LOWDOWN

I ate these snake skins in the Beijing Night Market in China where they are sold for the weirdness rather than the flavour. I wasn't worried by the skins themselves but the thought that maybe the flesh had been thrown away – there's no snake steak on sale. Of course, you only think that after you've eaten it.

ADULT NEEDED

SERVES: 4

KIT
Sharp knife and an adult to use it
Roasting tray
2 saucepans

INGREDIENTS
4 mini pumpkins or squash
Salt and pepper
8 tsp olive oil
100 g spaghetti, snapped
  into short pieces and cooked
  according to the instructions on
  the packet (or canned spaghetti
  if you're feeling really lazy!)
300 ml jar of tomato pasta sauce

MAGGOTY-BRAINED PUMPKIN HEADS

There's nothing quite like dipping a spoon into an open skull and scooping out the brains – sort of makes life worth living, don't you think? So, here's how to make your own.

   Around Hallowe'en you can often buy little squash called "hooligan" squash, which always tickles me.

METHOD
1. Preheat the oven to 180°C/gas 4. Wash the squash, then pat them dry and get an adult to carefully cut a small lid off the top (watch out

– the skin is tough and they can slip about). Scoop out the seeds with a teaspoon and discard.

2. Get your tame adult to carefully cut a scary face into the squash, making sure the cuts are mainly on the surface and aren't too large, or the fillings will leak out.

3. Lay the squash in a roasting tray and season the insides with salt and pepper. Put two teaspoons of olive oil inside each one and place the lids next to them, flat side down. Roast for 1 hour, or until the skins are just starting to brown.

4. Remove the squash from the oven and set aside to cool a little. Cook the spaghetti according to the instructions on the packet, heat the tomato sauce in a small pan and mix them together.

5. Carefully pour the pasta with sauce into the squash and put the lids back on. Serve with a witchy cackle.

GASTROTRUMPS
FIELD RAT

THE STATS

From: India

Taste: Young, tender
chicken   8/10

Smell: Burnt or smoky   5/10

Texture: Crispy skin and
tender flesh   7/10

Looks: Ratty   1/10

Adventure level:
Yikes   9/10

Nutritional value:
OK – similar to rabbit   8/10

£ Value: **Cheap as chips**

THE LOWDOWN

I stayed with a community known as the "rat-eaters" in a poor, rural part of India called Bihar. The workers have a deal with the landowners: if they catch any rats they can keep them to eat. The landowners get pest control, the workers get a little protein. The rat is cooked over a fire so that the fur can be scraped off.

ADULT NEEDED

KIT
A cheeky grown-up
Roasting tray

INGREDIENTS
Whole medium chicken
Splash of olive oil
Salt
Can of drink such as cola,
  lemonade or ginger beer
Sprig of rosemary or thyme
  (optional)

TOP TIP
Serve with roast potatoes,
broccoli, carrots and gravy.

CHICKEN WITH A CAN OF COLA UP ITS BUM

It's hard trying to keep meals interesting, especially when adults are so painfully unadventurous with their food. But if your folks are too boring to cook lamb's testicles or cow's brains and always resort to chicken, the least they can do is shove a bit of excitement into it.

This particular shoving might look like a rude thing to do to a chicken, but it's actually a brilliant way to cook it, as it stays lovely and moist inside. You can add some extra flavour to your gravy with a splash from the can. Cola is great for this, but lemonade, ginger beer and orangeade all work well.

METHOD
1. Take your chicken out of the fridge and leave it covered for 20 minutes, to come up to room temperature. While you are waiting, preheat the oven to 200°C/gas 6, and perhaps prepare some vegetables.

2. Wipe the chicken inside and out with some kitchen roll, then pour over a splash of olive oil. Throw a pinch of salt on, then rub it all over – don't be shy now, but do wash your hands thoroughly straight afterwards.

3. Drink about half of the can of drink, then stand it upright on a large roasting tray. Place the chicken straight onto the can – it may need a little bit of indecent shoving to get it on the can, but it should fit. Make sure it's nicely balanced – if it feels wobbly, wedge some other ovenproof bowls around it. If you've got some herbs handy, tuck them into the chicken anywhere you can.

4. Pop the chicken into the oven for 45 minutes, then reduce the temperature to 180°C/gas 4 for another 30 minutes. It'll need about 1¼ hours total. Remove the chicken from the oven and check that it's

cooked through by inserting a skewer into the thickest part of the leg. If the juices run clear, without any blood, then it's done. If not, pop it back in for another 10 minutes and check again.

5. Get an adult to help you extract the chicken from the can (beware it will be extremely hot) and use the hot liquid inside the can to help make a gravy.

6. With grown-up help, pop the hot chicken back on the empty can and set aside to rest for 20 minutes while you cook your vegetables.

7. Serve the whole thing on the table and carve.

KIT
2 big strong sealable freezer
  bags
A pair of gloves

INGREDIENTS
200 ml cream
20 g caster sugar
20 g strawberry jam
150 g salt
400 g crushed ice (put the ice in
  a plastic bag and whack it with
  a rolling pin to crush it up)

INSTANT ICE CREAM IN A BAG

Ever invited your mates over for a sneaky ice cream freezer-raid, only to discover that your even sneakier mum and dad scoffed the whole lot the night before? Parents can be so selfish sometimes, can't they? Well, never fear, I have the solution to all your chilled-dessert supply troubles. It's called Instant Ice Cream in a Bag.

This awesomely fast ice cream method uses a brilliantly twisted law of physics. When ice melts, the process is *endothermic*: basically, the change from solid ice to liquid water uses up energy in the form of heat. In this case, that heat is drawn from the ice cream mixture which becomes colder. Salty water has a lower freezing temperature than normal water, so the endothermic process draws so much heat energy so fast from the cream mixture that it freezes.

METHOD
1. Open up one of the freezer bags and pour in the cream, caster sugar and strawberry jam but NOT the salt!
2. Seal it REALLY TIGHTLY and set it aside.
3. In the other bag, add the salt and the crushed ice, then put in the tightly sealed bag full of the creamy mixture.
4. Now make sure you're wearing gloves and gently shake it. As the salt and ice mix, the temperature will drop quickly, and it'll start to chill your creamy mixture. It will get very, very cold. You don't need to shake it the whole time — it can just sit on a plate and chill out. After 3–5 minutes you should feel the mixture beginning to harden.
5. When it feels as though it's frozen really well, open up the outer bag and take out the inner bag. Rinse it under the tap to get rid of all the salt, then open up and dig in.

ADULT NEEDED

MAKES: 6 small jellies
(or 1 really big one)

KIT
An adult
UV light (a decent one, otherwise
the effect will be weak)
Large heatproof bowl
Scissors
Microwave
6 clear glasses (or one large
jelly mould)

INGREDIENTS
1 pack of leaf gelatine (enough to
set 1 litre of jelly)
1 litre tonic water, chilled
2 lemons, juiced
100 g caster sugar

FLUORESCENT JELLIES

Believe it or not, there are several different foods and drinks that naturally glow under fluorescent light, including peas, Marmite and my favourite: tonic water. Tonic water is amazing. The quinine in tonic water is anti-malarial, anti-inflammatory and reduces the effects of fevers. It's also one of the bitterest substances on earth, so it's fun to put in drinks. More importantly for me, quinine makes the jelly *fluoresce*: it will absorb invisible high-energy ultraviolet light and then re-emit it within a billionth of a second as visible lower-energy blue light. Put simply: it glows under UV light.

This is brilliant for parties. You do need to borrow a good UV lamp to get the effect, and it has to be served in the dark otherwise you can't see it glow. Tonic water can be an acquired taste, but if you add lemon juice and sugar, it's pretty good stuff.

METHOD
1. Check the instructions on the packet of gelatine and take out enough sheets to make up 1 litre of jelly. Cut the sheets into shreds with scissors and put them in a large heatproof bowl. Add 200 ml of tonic water to the bowl and leave it for 10 minutes to soften.

2. Put the bowl in a microwave and heat for 40–50 seconds, then add the sugar and stir until everything has completely dissolved. Now add the lemon juice.

3. Add the rest of the cold tonic water, pouring carefully so that you don't lose all those lovely bubbles.

4. Pour the liquid into glasses and put them in the fridge to set (this will take about 3 hours or so). If you're using a mould, make it easy to get the jelly out later by first putting a tiny bit of vegetable oil onto a piece of kitchen roll and lightly greasing the inside of the mould.

5. Serve at night. Put your UV light on the table and place the jellies as close to it as possible. Turn the regular lights off and watch those jellies glow!

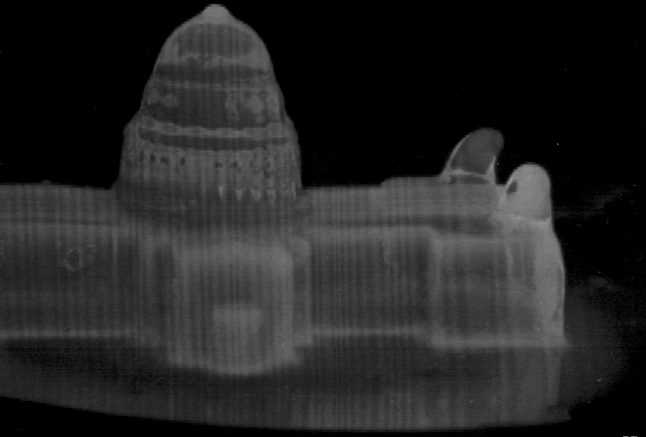

ADULT NEEDED

MAKES: 4 lollies

KIT

A sensible adult
Greaseproof or non-stick baking
  paper
Baking sheet or tray that will fit in
  your fridge
Small saucepan
Heatproof mixing bowl
4 lolly sticks (or old chopsticks)

INGREDIENTS

200 g bar of chocolate
Loads of sweets

CHOCOLATE CHAOS LOLLIES

Adults think that chocolate rots your brain, makes your legs turn mouldy and your eyeballs burst out of their sockets. Or something like that. Whatever the reason, they don't like kids eating it.

One easy way to get adults to let you have more chocolate is to be *creative* with it. The moment you say you're being *creative*, you can get away with anything. And the great thing about chocolate is that it melts when you heat it a little over room temperature and goes solid again pretty easily. So you can just buy a load of chocolate and with a bit of help melt it down, then turn it into a different *creative* shape and eat it. Bingo: Mum and Dad happy, you happy. Just make sure they don't realize that you're just doing this to eat more chocolate – talk about "the unifying structure of the architectural form" as you make a ridiculous mess of the kitchen.

METHOD

1. Lay a piece of greaseproof paper (or non-stick baking paper) on a baking sheet or tray that will fit in your fridge.
2. Put 5 cm or so of water into a small saucepan and ask your adult to put it on a medium heat. Place the heatproof bowl on top. In cooking lingo, this is called a *bain-marie* and is basically a way of heating something very gently.
3. Break the chocolate up into small pieces and put it in the bowl. Stir it gently as it melts, and as soon as it has melted take it off the heat.

4. Using a spoon, drop four small splodges of chocolate onto the paper and place the sticks onto them. Be careful – the chocolate will be very hot. Spread the rest of it on top of the sticks and around them, making sure that each shape is well connected to its stick. Crazy patterns are great, but make sure they're connected enough to hold together as a lolly.

5. Put the lollies in the fridge to set for 15 minutes.

6. When the lollies are fully set, peel the paper off and get stuck in.

THE STATS

From: Ivory Coast		
Taste: Bitter, nutty		2/10
Smell: Spicy		5/10
Texture: Crunchy coffee		4/10
Looks: Massive bean		5/10
Adventure level: Thank heavens someone tried it!		5/10
Nutritional Value: Vitamins and minerals		7/10
£ Value:		Pocket money

THE LOWDOWN

A cocoa pod contains 30–50 beans. Raw cocoa beans are a little nutty but mostly tasteless. Once they are fermented, dried, roasted and crushed, the cocoa nibs become really bitter. It's only after many processes (and sugar) that it becomes the chocolate we know and love. Proof that we have to experiment with our food to discover the best things on earth!

ANATOMY OF A FART

Farts are NOT wizards' cooking fuel, they have nothing to do with raspberries and they aren't funny. OK, that last one is a lie. But other than being very, very funny, what IS a fart? After all, a grown adult will drop about 24–30 clangers a day, which adds up to around two litres of gas. Let's talk fart.

Doctors call the special mix of gases in a fart flatus (pronounced "flart-oos"). Flatus is basically the combined gas created by billions and billions of tiny bacteria, which hang out in your large intestine in order to break down what's left of your food after it's been through your small intestine. The gas is a by-product of all their hard work.

Farts are mainly nitrogen (which isn't surprising when you consider that every breath of air we take is about 78% nitrogen) and carbon dioxide. There are small amounts of flammable methane and hydrogen, but the smell doesn't come from any of these. It comes from sulphur-based compounds such as hydrogen sulphide, dimethyl sulphide, methanethiol and skatole which give the glorious stench to a really good trouser-trumpet.

I'm not entirely sure why we're so embarrassed about farting, seeing as we ALL do it,

THE STATS

From: China
Taste: None to speak of   1/10
Smell: A little offally   2/10
Texture: Slimy and
crunchy   9/10
Looks: Undeniably
duck-webby   1/10
Adventure level: Come
on, be bold   7/10
Nutritional value: Good
gelatine   6/10
£ Value: Pocket money

THE LOWDOWN

Like so many foods from China
and Japan, this one is really
about the texture rather than the
taste. People love the way duck
feet feel in the mouth – both
soft and slimy yet strangely
cartilaginous. The taste comes
from whichever sauce they have
been cooked in – I prefer a hot-
sweet chilli sauce, but black bean
sauce is good too.

and we have no choice in the
matter. If you didn't fart, you'd
either explode or the gas could
travel back up through your
digestive system and cause all
manner of problems. My farts
are particularly pleasant. Well,
I think so.

ADULT NEEDED

MAKES: 4 portions

KIT
An adult
Chopping knife
Large bowl
4 serving bowls

INGREDIENTS
Use any fruit, such as grapes,
  strawberries, bananas,
  blackberries, kiwi fruit,
  pineapple (fresh or canned
  and drained of syrup)
Plain yoghurt (optional)
2 packets of popping candy

TOP TIP
You need to sprinkle the
popping candy on the fruit
at the last minute otherwise it
might dissolve and disappear
before you serve it.

POPPING CANDY FRUIT SALAD

I love sprinkling popping candy as a topping on desserts
and fruit salads. It always comes as a shock to people if you
don't tell them beforehand!

METHOD
1. Ask an adult to help you cut the strawberries and
grapes in half, the banana into bite-sized pieces
and skin and chop the pineapple into
small chunks. Put them all into a
large bowl and mix them
together.

2. Put a serving of chopped fruit into each bowl, then drop a splodge of yoghurt (if you're using it) on top.
3. Scatter the popping candy over the fruit salad and serve immediately.

ADULT NEEDED

SERVES: 4

KIT
An unsuspecting adult
Knife
Peeler
Frying pan

INGREDIENTS
200 g Jerusalem
    artichokes, peeled
½ lemon
330 g can of cooked
    flageolet beans
100 g Brussels sprouts
100 g streaky bacon
1 tbsp olive oil
1 tbsp very finely sliced onion

For the dressing:
Splash of wine vinegar
1 tsp honey
½ tsp French mustard
Pinch of salt and pepper

MICROFACT

THE MOST NOTORIOUS COMPONENT OF
FARTS IS THE GAS SKATOLE, WHICH
IS RESPONSIBLE FOR THEIR STRONG
POO-EY SMELL. HOWEVER, IN SMALL
CONCENTRATIONS IT SMELLS DELICIOUS
AND IS PART OF THE SCENT PROFILE
OF JASMINE AND ORANGE FLOWERS.

THE WORLD'S FARTIEST MEAL

Now that we know why we fart, we can find a practical use for our knowledge (isn't that what education is all about?) by cooking food that makes people fart.

Don't tell your diners that you're making them a flatulent meal – that would ruin the fun. Just feed them the fartiest foods you can find, and sit back and wait. It can take anywhere between 1 and 8 hours for the effects to be felt. For me, it takes less than an hour from eating Jerusalem artichokes to land squarely in the pump zone. Oh, yes!

You'll need an adult to help with the chopping and boiling. Just don't tell them what the project's about.

METHOD

1. With the help of an adult slice your Jerusalem artichokes really thinly and place them in a bowl. Squeeze the lemon over them and toss them around in the juice (this will stop them going brown).

2. Drain and rinse the flageolet beans in cold water and add them to the Jerusalem artichokes.

3. Slice the bases off the Brussels sprouts and discard, then chop them in half.

4. Get your grown-up to help chop the bacon into little pieces and place in a frying pan on a medium heat with the olive oil and sprouts. Fry them for about 8 minutes until the bacon starts to get a bit crispy.

5. Add the bacon and Brussels sprouts to the bowl along with the onion. Mix the salad dressing ingredients together in a cup or jam jar, then pour it over the salad and mix everything together. Serve with some nice crusty bread, then just sit back and wait.

65

ADULT NEEDED

KIT

1 willing grown-up with decent
 DIY skills
Large, very tough, clean
 plastic bag
Empty water butt or large
 watertight bin
Chicken wire
2 pieces of wood 1 m long and
 4 cm x 4 cm wide
Clean piece of wood 1 m long
 and 5 cm x 1 cm wide
Pliers, saw, staplegun, cable ties,
 hammer, screws, screwdriver

INGREDIENTS

30 litres of made up squash
 (usually takes about 3 litres of
 concentrate, but make it up to
 your taste)
30 x 3 kg bags of ice (or enough
 to fill your bin or water butt)
30 kg salt
Chocolate sauce and sprinkles

TOP TIP

Read this all the way
through before you start
making it – it's pretty
involved. You'll need a bit of
cash for the ingredients, and
because you need a lot of
kit, you really need someone
who's great at DIY, problem-
solving and woodwork. Oh,
and do a bit of scheduling –
it takes 10 hours or so to set.

HOW TO MAKE A MEGALOLLY

The main problem with making massive ice lollies is that you need massive freezers. However, now that you and I have shared the joys of making Instant Ice Cream in a Bag (p. 54), I think we can break free of our refrigeration-related shackles and reach for the lolly skies. If we can make a mould big enough, we can use the ice-and-salt chilling reaction to freeze something HUGE.

   This is good for charity events, especially at school, when you need to do something spectacular to squeeze some cash out of those grown-ups for a good cause. But it's a bit tricky and you'll need a fair amount of kit – you'll also need the help of an adult who's pretty handy at DIY.

METHOD

1. First you need to make the ice lolly mould. Lay your strong plastic bag on the floor and cut it lengthways so that it's about 35 cm wide. Tape the cut sides back together with very strong tape. (A long but thin shape is best for efficient freezing, otherwise it will take days to set.) Get your grown-up to make an open-topped cage out of the chicken wire for it to sit in.

2. Ask your adult to fix the top of the chicken wire to the two strips of wood so that the top of the mould is level with the top of the bin or water butt. They can use staples or cable ties, but this does need to be pretty strong as it will hold a lot of water.

3. Open up the bag and fit it into the chicken wire mould. The bag should fill the cage without any wrinkles. Tape the top of the bag to the wooden frame so that it is held open and doesn't slip around.

4. Lower the frame into the bin or water butt. It should sit hanging down, with lots of space around it. Fill it with the made-up squash. Put the large thin stick into the squash for a lolly stick.

5. Fill the space around the lolly mould with ice and throw in about ¼ of the salt as you go. Mix them together with a spare piece of wood. The temperature will start to drop.

6. You'll need to keep adding ice and salt to the bin throughout the day in order to keep the temperature low enough for long enough. Because all lolly moulds will be different and bins are different sizes its hard to tell you exactly how long it will take or how much ice and salt you'll need. It took us about 10 hours to make the one in the photo.

7. Cover it in instant-setting chocolate sauce and sprinkles.

ADULT NEEDED

MAKES: 12 cupcakes

KIT
A well-behaved adult
Food processor or mixer
Cupcake baking tin
Paper cupcake cases
Small mixing bowl

INGREDIENTS
For the cupcakes:
150 g caster sugar
150 g butter
3 medium eggs
1 tsp vanilla flavouring
½ tsp of red food colouring
  (optional)
150 g self-raising flour

For the icing:
350 g icing sugar
75 g butter (taken out of the
  fridge 15 minutes before use)
300 g cream cheese
1 tsp vanilla flavouring
½ tsp green food colouring

SNOT CAKES

Let's face it: these are really just cupcakes. So far, so booooooring. But by using a good slug of food colouring, we can make them into something that looks really snotty. Yay!

METHOD

1. Ask your grown-up to turn the oven on to 180°C/gas 4 so that it heats up while you prepare the cake mixture.

2. Put the sugar, butter, eggs, vanilla and red food colouring into the food processor and with help, mix them up until nice and smooth.

3. Add the flour to the mixture and ask your well-behaved adult to whizz it in short bursts, but only until it has just mixed in (you can easily overblend this).

4. Lay your paper cases out on the baking tin, then divide the mixture between the cases. Each case should be about ⅔ full.

5. With your adult's help, put them in the middle of the oven and bake for 20 minutes. Check them after 15 minutes, just in case they are ready early!

6. While they are baking, make your icing: wipe the food processor bowl clean and add the icing sugar, butter, cream cheese and flavouring. Whizz it up until nicely mixed, then drop some green food colouring in and mix with a fork until nicely snot-coloured. Put it in a bowl and keep in the fridge to chill.

7. When the cupcakes are nicely browned, ask your grown-up to take them out of the oven. Then leave them to cool for 20 minutes on a cooling rack, if you have one.

8. Build a big ugly green icing bogey on top of each cupcake to give them a really disgusting appearance.

HOW TO GROW A SQUARE WATERMELON

This isn't just a clever bit of photo-manipulation. You really can grow square watermelons. Once the watermelon has started to grow normally and healthily in the field, a glass (or plastic) cube is slipped over it. As the watermelon continues to grow, it squashes against the glass, and is literally forced into a cube shape, with just the twiggy bit at the top poking out. When it's filled the entire glass, it's taken out before the glass breaks. It's a lot of effort for a bit of fruit.

What's the point? So that it fits in your fridge better? So that it doesn't roll around in the back of the car? So that they can be stacked better? No. It's just a bit of fun, and I must admit I find them very cool indeed, even though they taste identical to a normal watermelon. They are expensive, though. Around £70 if you want to import one. We got them sent over from Taiwan for filming. Pointless, yes, but fascinating and fun.

WHEN FOOD AID TURNS BAD

When we hear about hunger in poor countries, our natural reaction is to want to send food. Well, it makes complete sense, doesn't it? "You need food. We have some to spare. Have some of ours."

Trouble is, it's not that simple. I've been to Haiti, Ethiopia and northern Uganda where food aid has caused massive problems. When food is handed out for free or sold very cheaply, local farmers can't sell the food they have managed to produce, however little there might be. After all, who in their right mind would pay for food when you can have it for free? So the local farmers can't sell the crops they've grown, and then they don't make enough money to buy seed, fertilizer or labour to plant and harvest next season's crop. So what happens? Next year, there's even less food to go around because the farmers couldn't afford to grow anything, and the region is even hungrier than it was before. It's a vicious circle and in places like Haiti where American rice is so much cheaper than

locally-produced rice, it can turn into a devastating cycle of dependency.

These days, food aid agencies like the UN's World Food Programme are getting wise to the problems that food aid can create and they run "work for food" programmes so that food isn't given for free, but has to

be earned. They often manage to buy it from local farmers too, which can help. It seems a shame that generosity can be complicated, but food is always so much more than just a bag of calories – the less you have of it, the more important, and the more complicated it becomes.

ADULT NEEDED

SERVES: 20

KIT

A crispy adult
Very large saucepan
Wooden spoon
Very large mixing bowl
Baking tray
Cocktail sticks

INGREDIENTS

260 g butter
2 x 300 g pots golden syrup
1 x 400 g tub drinking
  chocolate powder
4 boxes rice crispies
Butter or oil for greasing
Sweets

MASSIVE CHOCOLATE RICE CRISPY HEAD

Do you get bored of food that comes in neat portions? Me too. If you're having your mates around for a party, why not make one MAAAssive chocolate head and let everyone just dive in and make a mess?

   This recipe uses golden syrup and drinking chocolate powder instead of melted chocolate because it helps the head set really easily. You could simply use melted chocolate, but it sometimes goes soggy, so it's difficult to use just chocolate to make a MAAAssive head.

METHOD

1. Do this one box of rice crispies at a time, otherwise it's really difficult to stir without mashing everything! Put ¼ of your butter (65 g) in a very large saucepan and with an adult on stand-by put it on a very gentle heat. Pour in 150 g golden syrup and mix in 100 g drinking chocolate powder. Stir until it has all melted into a sticky chocolate sauce, and turn the heat straight off (otherwise it'll be too hot to handle). Tip in one box of rice crispies and gently mix it all together using a wooden spoon.

2. Take your very large mixing bowl (the biggest you can find) and grease it with a little extra butter on a piece of kitchen roll – this will be the mould for your head, so make sure it'll fit in the fridge.

3. Tip the first batch of rice crispy mix into the bowl and press it down firmly around the bottom and sides of the bowl.

4. Make up another batch of chocolatey crispsies to the same recipe: 65 g butter, 150 g golden syrup, 100 g chocolate powder, 1 box rice crispies. Heat until melted but not too hot and stir. Tip it into the bowl to make another layer.

5. Now do the same again for the next two batches, packing it all in. If you have any left-over mix, use it to make individual heads in cake cases.

6. When the bowl is completely full, flatten the top with your hands and pop it in the fridge to set for a couple of hours.

7. To give your head a face, place a baking tray over the top of the bowl and flip the whole thing upside down. Your giant rice crispy head should come out in one giant head-shaped piece. Give it eyes, a nose, a mouth and ears by attaching sweets with the cocktail sticks. Don't worry if it's not perfect – the sheer scale of this will blow everyone away.

8. If you're not going to eat it straight away, keep it in the fridge.

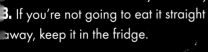

KIT
Whisk – hand held or electric
Mixing bowl
Rolling pin
Big serving dish

INGREDIENTS
600 ml double cream
4 small ready-made meringues
250 g strawberries
250 g raspberries
1 pack jelly babies
100 g chocolate buttons

TOP TIP
If you can get your folks to let you, you can build this straight onto a clean table, without putting it on a plate first – then everyone can dig in with a fork. It's a classic Italian way of eating called "alla spianatora". Heck, you're going to clean the table anyway – why not have some fun with it!

MICROFACT
JELLY SWEETS ARE USUALLY MADE FROM BONES. THE GELATINE IN THEM IS MADE BY BOILING ANIMAL BONES TO EXTRACT THE STUFF THAT MAKES SWEETS STICKY AND CHEWY. THAT'S WHY VEGETARIANS DON'T EAT THEM.

INCREDIBLE MESS

This naughty dish is based on the famous 200-year-old dessert called Eton Mess. It's traditionally served at the annual cricket match between Eton and Winchester, two of the world's poshest schools.

The great thing about Eton Mess is that it's simply a mix of delicious things like strawberries, whipped cream and meringue, mashed together into a mess. Genius. Basically you can use anything you like to make Incredible Mess, but to make it look really cool, don't mix it into a slurry – otherwise it will look like puke. Less is more. Trust me.

METHOD
1. Put the double cream into a bowl and whip it until it's good and stiff using a whisk. (Just so you know – whipping is a way of mixing thousands of tiny bubbles of air into cream to make it seem solid.) Leave the whipped cream in the bowl.
2. Put the meringues onto a chopping board and bash them into bite-sized chunks using a rolling pin, then gently stir them into the cream.
3. Either on a plate or (if your folks let you) straight on the table, build a great big creamy hill of mess.
4. Chop the strawberries in half and then stick them, together with the raspberries, jelly babies and chocolate buttons into the cream. Now dive in!

ADULT NEEDED

KIT
A grown-up
Knife
Small saucepan
Heatproof bowl
Wooden spoon
Greaseproof paper

INGREDIENTS
1 carton of ripe strawberries,
  chilled (about 350g)
200g white chocolate
2 tubes of ready-made red icing
Handful of blueberries, halved

MICROFACT

DOES CHEWING-GUM REALLY TAKE
7 YEARS TO DIGEST? NAH. THAT
WAS JUST MADE UP TO SCARE YOU.
IT'S INDIGESTIBLE, BUT THAT'S NOT
NECESSARILY BAD - VEGETABLES
CONTAIN HEALTHY INDIGESTIBLE
FIBRE WHICH IS GOOD FOR YOUR POO.
MASSIVE AMOUNTS COULD CREATE
A GUT BLOCKAGE, BUT IT'S VERY RARE.

WHITE CHOCOLATE STRAWBERRY EYEBALLS

Nyaa hah hah hah HAAAAAAAAAAAH! HAAAAAAH!
Oops – sorry. I got a bit carried away there.

These are a great treat for Hallowe'en, not just because
they look like eyeballs, but also because when you bite into
them, the strawberry looks like the flesh inside an eyeball.
Nya haaa hah HAAAAH! Oops. There I go again.

METHOD

1. Wash and dry the strawberries. Pull any greenery off the top of
the strawberry. Slice the top off the thin pointy end of each one
(so that they will stand upright). Pop them back in the fridge to keep
them well chilled.

2. Add a few centimetres of water to a small saucepan and, with
your grown-up on hand, put it on a low heat. Put a heatproof bowl
over the top so it sits above the hot water.

3. Now break the chocolate into small chunks and add it to the warm
bowl! Melt it slowly, mixing with a wooden spoon. Do this with an
adult and don't go too fast or boil it – the chocolate will turn grainy.
Take the bowl off the heat as soon as the chocolate has melted and
test it carefully to make sure the chocolate won't burn your fingers.

4. Dip the strawberries in and completely cover them with chocolate,
then place them on some greaseproof paper with the big rounded
end facing upwards. Leave to set.

5. When the chocolate is solid, draw scary veins on your eyeballs
with the red icing and then top each one off with a halved blueberry.
Place in the fridge for 15 minutes or until you're ready to serve them.

ADULT NEEDED

MAKES: 24 bars

KIT

A sweet-toothed adult
30 cm x 20 cm Swiss roll tin
(or a shallow roasting tray)
2 bowls
2 saucepans
Small, clean, dry paintbrush

INGREDIENTS

For the shortbread:
250 g plain flour
75 g caster sugar
175 g butter, softened (by taking
it out of the fridge for 15 minutes
before starting to cook)

For the caramel:
100 g butter
100 g caster sugar (or light
muscavado sugar, if you've got
some)
2 x 397 g cans condensed milk

For the topping:
200 g plain or milk chocolate,
broken into pieces
12 sheets loose leaf edible
gold

MICROFACT

CAN YOU EAT GOLD?
YES, BUT ONLY SMALL AMOUNTS OF
FOOD-GRADE GOLD LEAF, NOT YOUR
MUM'S JEWELLERY. IT'S A PERMITTED
FOOD ADDITIVE CALLED E175, AND
YOU CAN ALSO EAT TINY AMOUNTS OF
SILVER, OR E174.

BILLIONAIRE'S SHORTBREAD

This is a recipe for cooking with pure gold. Yes, it's bizarre. Yes, it's ridiculous. And yes, it's bonkers. But if you're having a party and you want to cook something out of this world, this baby's for you. At 50p per slice, it's not actually that expensive, considering that if you serve this to your mates, they will never forget it! You can buy gold leaf in books of 25 sheets from art materials shops, and it's beaten so amazingly thin that there's actually not that much gold in each sheet, which is why it doesn't cost as much as you might think. Be careful with it – it disintegrates if you touch it with your fingers and it's so light that it floats away easily. (Don't buy the stuff called "transfer leaf" as it's too difficult to use.)

This ridiculously indulgent snack is usually called millionaire's shortbread because it tastes so rich, but with a coating of gold, I think it's fair to call it billionaire's shortbread.

METHOD

1. While you lightly grease a Swiss roll tin by coating a piece of kitchen roll in butter and wiping it all over the inside of the tin, get your handy adult to preheat the oven to 180°C/gas 4.
2. Make the shortbread. Put the flour and caster sugar in a big bowl and mix them together. Then add the butter and rub it all together using your fingertips, until it looks like fine breadcrumbs – this'll probably take 3–5 minutes. Then squeeze it all into a ball and knead it on a clean surface for a couple of minutes by squashing it with the base of your palm, then turning it and squishing it again. It will form a big lump of dough. Press the dough into the base of the tin and spread it all around so it makes an even layer.

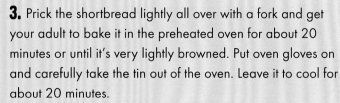

3. Prick the shortbread lightly all over with a fork and get your adult to bake it in the preheated oven for about 20 minutes or until it's very lightly browned. Put oven gloves on and carefully take the tin out of the oven. Leave it to cool for about 20 minutes.

4. Now for the caramel. Make sure you have an adult to help you – it will be very, very hot. First, put the butter, sugar and condensed milk into a saucepan and heat gently until the sugar has dissolved. Bring to the boil, stirring all the time, then reduce the heat to as low as possible and simmer very gently, stirring continuously, for about 5 minutes or until the mixture has thickened a little. Pour this caramel over the shortbread (flatten it with a knife if necessary) and leave to cool again.

5. Now the topping. Fill a small saucepan ¼ full with water and, with help, put it on a medium heat, then place a heatproof bowl on top of it. Add the chocolate and stir it slowly until it has all melted through. Pour the melty chocolate over the caramel (spreading it to the edges with a knife) and leave it to set, but not in the fridge. (If it's too cold, it's very hard to get the gold to stick to it.)

6. When it has set, very gently layer the gold on top, one sheet at a time, using the backing paper (not your fingers!) to press it down onto the chocolate. The warmth of your skin through the paper should be enough to stick the gold to the chocolate, so go slowly and have patience. Use a soft paintbrush if you need to and keep going until the whole slab is covered.

7. Cut your billionaire's shortbread into 24 bars.

ADULT NEEDED

MAKES: 4 small cups

KIT
A sensible adult
Knife
Small saucepan
Wooden spoon

INGREDIENTS
1 mild red chilli (or half
   a hot one)
600 ml full-fat milk
100 g plain chocolate
100 ml double cream

REALLY HOT CHOCOLATE

Chocolate drinks were first made about 2,000 years ago by the Mayans in South America. They, and the Aztecs who came later, drank cocoa-based drinks, but these were not like ours – they mixed the cocoa with chilli, water and cornmeal. I've drunk hot chocolate made with water and cornmeal in Mexico and it's ... erm ... OK, but the chilli is a brilliant addition.

METHOD
1. With your adult's help, slice the chilli in half, scrape out and throw away the seeds, and put it in a saucepan. Wash your hands carefully after you touch the chilli. Pour over the milk and (with an adult on stand-by) heat gently on a medium heat. As soon as it starts to simmer, turn the heat off and leave it to sit. The chilli will start to flavour the milk.

2. Meanwhile, break the chocolate up into chunks and bash them to pieces with a rolling pin.

3. Remove the chilli from the milk and throw it away. Add the cream and chocolate and heat the milk up again, stirring so that the chocolate melts. Turn it off just before it reaches simmering point.

4. Leave to cool for a minute or two, then share the drink out between four cups. You can garnish it with another chilli and some whipped cream if you fancy.

ADULT NEEDED

MAKES: 2 glasses of
each flavour

KIT
A superfly adult
Blender or food processor

INGREDIENTS

Strawberry and banana:
1 handful of strawberries (with
   their green tops taken off)
1 peeled banana
75 ml Greek yoghurt
200 ml milk
1 tbsp honey

Mango and banana:
1 mango, peeled, stone removed
   and chopped into chunks
1 peeled banana
75 ml Greek yoghurt
200 ml milk
1 tbsp honey

Blueberry:
1 handful of blueberries
1 peeled banana
75 ml Greek yoghurt
200 ml milk
1 tbsp honey

MICROFACT

ORANGES ARE HIGHLY
FLAMMABLE - OR AT LEAST THE
LIMONENE IN THEIR ZEST IS. DRIED
ORANGE PEEL MAKES BRILLIANT
FIRELIGHTERS.

SMOOOOOOTHIES

Chalax juice. Dead easy. Very very tasty.

METHOD
1. With your adult's help, put all the ingredients into a
blender and whizz until smooth.
2. Erm ... that's it.

GASTROTRUMPS
COCKSCOMBS

THE STATS
From: UK
Taste: Lightly meaty — 6/10
Smell: Boiled chicken — 5/10
Texture: Soft and slimy — 2/10
Looks: Soft and squidgy — 3/10
Adventure level:
Takes real gastro-guts — 9/10
Nutritional value:
Fatty but good protein. — 6/10
£ Value: Big treat

THE LOWDOWN
Cockscombs are the wibbly-wobbly bits on chickens' heads. When chickens are butchered, the cockscombs are normally discarded or used in mechanically-recovered meat products like hot dogs and burgers. However, they are also seen as a luxury ingredient by some of the finest offal restaurants.

ADULT NEEDED

KIT
A bubbly adult
Large saucepan with a lid
Non-stick baking tray
Wooden spoon

INGREDIENTS
A small lump of butter
300 g caster sugar
150 ml golden syrup
2 tbsp glucose syrup
1 tbsp white wine vinegar
2 tsp bicarbonate of soda

FIZZY HONEYCOMB

This is a bonkers recipe – it all seems a bit dull until you add the bicarbonate of soda, then all hell breaks loose!

This recipe involves boiling sugar, which can be very dangerous as it gets SO hot. You MUST get an adult to help you with this.

METHOD

1. Grease the baking tray by putting a lump of butter on it, and spreading it around with a piece of kitchen roll.

2. Put the sugar, golden syrup, glucose syrup, vinegar and 100 ml water into a large saucepan and get your adult to put it on a low heat. Stir until the sugar has dissolved (this is really important). Put the lid on the pan and let it simmer gently for 2 minutes.

3. Ask your grown-up to remove the lid, turn the heat up a little and boil it until the liquid has turned dark brown and reached hard-crack stage (150°C). This can take 15–30 minutes and must be watched at all times to make sure it doesn't boil over. To test for the hard-crack stage get your adult to dip a teaspoon into the mixture and drop a blob of it into a glass of cold water. If you're at hard-crack stage, it should turn hard and brittle. If it's still a bit sticky, you're not at hard-crack yet and the honeycomb WILL NOT WORK. You need to keep on boiling it for a few more minutes.

4. When the mixture is ready, turn off the heat and stir in the bicarbonate of soda with a wooden spoon. This is when it all goes nuts! The mixture will start to fizz up and expand. (Which is why you need a large saucepan). While it's foaming, quickly pour the mixture onto the greased baking tray and then leave it somewhere cool and dry to set – this can take a good hour or two. But bear in mind that this honeycomb is hygroscopic – it will slowly absorb moisture from the air and go sticky.

5. When it has set, break it into chunks. If you can manage not to eat them all straight away, store the chunks in an airtight container.

WHY AND HOW TO EAT A VIDEO CAMERA

I once ate a small video camera called a Pillcam to film my entire digestive system. I was making a TV programme about what happens after you've eaten your lunch, and although I've eaten some weird things, this was pretty freaky. The Pillcam was about half the size of your thumb (big for a pill, but small for a video camera), and it's got a little flashing light so that it can film inside the murky world of your guts (there are mine, on the right), wirelessly sending the footage to a computer.

After you've eaten your lunch, it starts an incredible journey through you. Your body breaks down the food and extracts as much nutrition from it as possible, before getting rid of what remains safely and cleanly.

When the pillcam has gone through your body, you poo it out. Don't worry, you don't need to fish it out of the toilet – it's disposable!

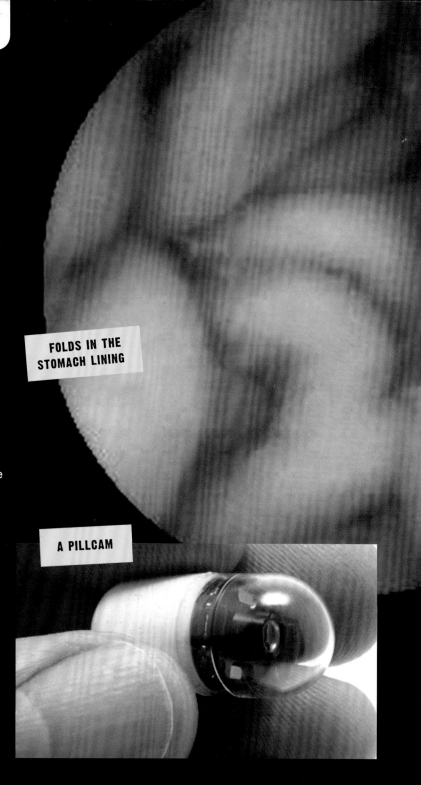

FOLDS IN THE STOMACH LINING

A PILLCAM

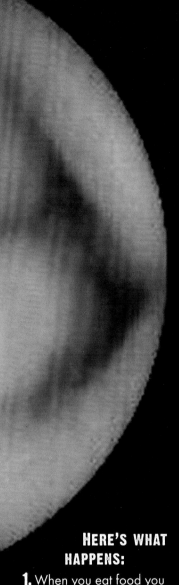

which kills most bacteria and breaks down your food even more. Food stays in here for an hour or two and ends up as a gloopy liquid called chyme.

3. Next stop is the small intestine, which is an odd name for something that's about 7 metres long. Food is squashed along this long tube, and is mixed with enzymes (chemicals made in your pancreas that break your food down so you can extract the nutrients). About 95% of digestion happens along this section.

4. What's left then enters the large intestine, which is only 1.5 metres long but much wider. Food will stay here for up to 16 hours, while the bacteria in your guts break it down (creating farts as a by-product) and let you absorb vitamins from it. Most of the water left in the food is extracted here, and what's left is poo.

5. There you go. If your folks moan about this book being a bit naughty, show them this explanation and tell them that it has made you a better person and you'll probably become a prime minister or brain surgeon or something.

HERE'S WHAT HAPPENS:

1. When you eat food you begin to break it down by chewing it and mixing it with saliva.

2. After you swallow, it goes down your oesophagus into your stomach, which is basically a holding chamber full of vicious hydrocholoric acid,

GASTROTRUMPS
CANE RAT

THE STATS
From: Cameroon
Taste: Sweet, slightly gamey meat   **10/10**
Smell: Clean and porky   **8/10**
Texture: Moist and succulent   **9/10**
Looks: Massive rabbit   **7/10**
Adventure level: Tastes too good to be scared   **4/10**
Nutrition: Similar to chicken   **7/10**
£ Value: **Pocket Money**

THE LOWDOWN
The best meat I have EVER tasted. Cameroon has a huge problem with bushmeat. People love eating wild animals, some of which are endangered, such as monkeys, pythons, pangolins and even gorillas. So an enterprising bunch of businessmen set up a cane rat farm to provide bushmeat that doesn't need to be taken from the wild. Good news all around.

ADULT NEEDED

MAKES: 8 kebabs

KIT
An oven-ready adult
2 large bowls
8 x 15 cm kebab sticks (soaked in
  water for a few minutes first so
  they don't burn on the BBQ)
Sieve (optional)
Blazing hot BBQ (in summer)
  or a ridged grill-pan (in winter)

INGREDIENTS
Juice of ½ lemon
2 pears or apples
½ pineapple (or a can of
  pineapple chunks, well drained)
¼ large watermelon
2 tbsp olive oil
2 tbsp icing sugar (optional)
Mint, chopped (optional)

MICROFACT
APPLES CONTAIN A POISON CALLED
CYANIDE. BUT NOT A LOT. IT'S MAINLY
IN THEIR PIPS AND YOU'D NEED TO
EAT TRUCKLOADS TO REALLY POISON
YOURSELF.

FRUIT KEBABS

Grilled fruit! "What new culinary craziness is this?" I hear you cry. But no, I'm deadly serious. I know that fruit is often great as it is: pure, raw and naked as the day it was born. (Or grown. Whatever.) And there's nothing wrong with kebabulating it just like that. But sometimes it's good to give a hunk of pear, pineapple or watermelon a good roasting on a blazing hot grill-pan or BBQ. The sugars in fruit will caramelize under intense heat and turn into little specks of toffee, making the fruit taste even better than it did before.

Trouble is, you need a short sharp shock of blazing heat and no more. If you heat it for a long time under a weak heat you're not grilling fruit – you're making jam.

I do this in winter on a ridged grill-pan, but the best time and place to do this is on a summer BBQ while the charcoal is blazing hot. It can be a bit dangerous, so you will need the help and full attention of an oven-ready adult.

METHOD
1. Squeeze the lemon juice into a bowl. (This is to stop the cut fruit from going brown.) Core the pears or apples but don't bother to peel them. Chop them into 2 cm chunks, drop them into the lemon juice and toss them around. Chop all the other fruit into 2 cm cubes and add them to the pears or apples. Then add the olive oil and toss the fruit around until coated. Skewer the fruit on the soaked kebab sticks in a random order. Hold a sieve over the kebabs and shake a little dusting of icing sugar over all them. (This bit's optional, but makes the fruit even sweeter and more toffee-like.)
2. With your oven-ready adult to help you, grill or BBQ the kebabs for about 5–10 minutes on a very high heat, turning regularly, until a little browned all over. Allow to cool for a few minutes and serve either as a starter or dessert, with a little mint if you have some.

CRAZY

EXPERIMENTS

KIT

1 plastic food container with a lid
Egg
Spirit vinegar (although you could use malt vinegar too)

WHAT'S REALLY HAPPENING

The acid in the vinegar reacts with the calcium carbonate in the hard eggshell. This reaction breaks down the eggshell, giving off carbon dioxide (see the bubbles in the photo) and water as well as a chemical called calcium acetate. It leaves behind the semi-permeable membrane.

HOW TO MAKE A NAKED EGG

This is a pretty darn cool way to transform an egg into ... well ... something more than an egg. The experiment takes about 2 days, so you'll have to negotiate with your mum and dad to get a spot in the kitchen. Brush aside their objections by telling them that you're working for the cause of science and the future. Having messed up the planet with their cars and global warming, they'll have to let you tinker with a few experiments to help make everything better. That should crack it.

You can dissolve the shell of a raw egg using vinegar, which leaves you with a whole raw naked egg, which is very cool. When you pour vinegar over an egg, a reaction starts. You will see bubbles which start to form on the shell.

The reaction keeps going until all that's left of the shell is the semi-permeable membrane (a sort of skin that holds the egg together). You'll probably have noticed this odd thin skin inside an egg if you've ever had one boiled (with soldiers, natch).

Remember to always wash your hands carefully after handling raw eggs to avoid any problems from bacteria.

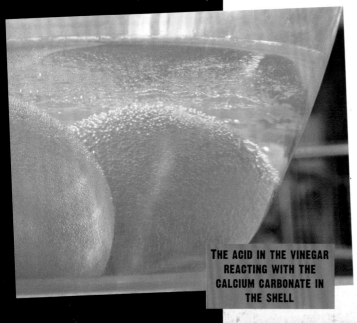

THE ACID IN THE VINEGAR REACTING WITH THE CALCIUM CARBONATE IN THE SHELL

METHOD

1. Place the egg in the plastic container. Pour in the vinegar until the egg is completely covered, then put the lid on.

2. Look closely. If little bubbles are beginning to form on the eggshell, then your chemical reaction has begun! Now leave the egg for 24 hours.

3. Take a look in the container. It should start to look murky. Leave the egg for a further 24 hours

4. After about 2 days, the shell will have completely dissolved, leaving behind a squidgy, squishy naked egg. Remove the egg from the vinegar and carefully rinse it with water. You now have a whole soft, raw egg. How cool is that? Once you've had enough fun mucking about with the naked egg, see how strong the membrane is by squeezing it until it bursts – over a sink, please...

GASTROTRUMPS
1000-YEAR-OLD EGG

THE STATS
From: China
Taste: Great – complex and nicely eggy   **7/10**
Smell: Your grandad's farts   **1/10**
Texture: Boiled egg crossed with jelly   **8/10**
Looks:
Rotten egg from hell   **2/10**
Adventure level:
It's that smell!   **8/10**
Nutritional value: Pretty good – for a rotten egg   **6/10**
£ Value: **Big treat**

THE LOWDOWN
These eggs taste great but smell bloomin' awful. They are duck eggs, preserved in ash, lime, clay and salt for a month or so. This changes their structure, colour and flavour and, once preserved, they last for ages.

WHAT DID ROMAN GLADIATORS EAT?

Roman gladiators ate huge amounts of simple carbohydrates in the form of gruel. This was a kind of savoury porridge, made from barley, beans and oats, all stewed in goat's milk. It was high in fibre and contained everything they needed to stay fighting fit, as well as having the added bonus of making them rather farty. To get extra calcium into their mainly vegetable-based diet, gladiators may have eaten charred wood or burnt bones. Niiiice.

If a gladiator wasn't hacked to pieces in the arena, he might win his freedom and a feast fit for an emperor. Often, the victory banquet included a suckling pig, a spectacular and very expensive delicacy. The most important guest would be offered the pig's ear, which rather strangely, was thought to be the best bit. And if you thought that was odd, rich Romans also loved to eat peacock tongues, roast dormice and boiled flamingo. There's no accounting for taste.

GASTROTRUMPS
EDIBLE FLIES

THE STATS

From: Mexico		
Taste: Not a lot		1/10
Smell: Marshy		1/10
Texture: Crunchy		7/10
Looks: Floor sweepings		1/10
Adventure level:		
Very cool.		10/10
Nutritional value:		
Bit of protein		4/10
£ Value:		Big treat

THE LOWDOWN

These little marsh flies come from the same lake as the edible fly eggs on p.15. The flies are mixed with eggs into an odd, unpalatable slurry. They are pretty much flavourless and are really eaten for the historical experience rather than the taste – the ancient Mayans used to be very fond of them.

WHAT ON EARTH ARE CALORIES?

Grown-ups often bang on about calories and how you shouldn't have too many of them. This isn't a bad piece of advice, but have you ever heard a grown-up come up with a believable explanation of what the energy in food actually is? Me neither.

Take a look at the photo above. Those, my friend, are calories. In this experiment, which was performed under controlled conditions, I am burning off the energy (or "calories") contained in a teaspoon of custard powder. The same amount of energy that you can see being released here, is released inside you when you eat and then metabolise (or burn up) a teaspoon of custard. It just happens more slowly inside you, and with less danger of taking your eyebrows off.

Do not even think about attempting this at home as it's complex and extremely dangerous.

HOW MANY KIDS DOES IT TAKE TO SMASH AN EGG?

KIT

A tray of 24–30 eggs (keep the
tray – it's important)
A friend or two to help you
A pair of clean trainers on your
feet – not your best shoes!

TOP TIP
Don't do this barefoot as
eggshells are sharp and can
cut your feet.

Eggs are amazing. Why? Well, they are packed with
everything a baby bird needs for the first stages of life, all
squeezed into a near-perfect oval shell. And what about that
shell? Well, it's pretty brittle, and can easily crack, as you'll
probably know if you've ever packed them at the bottom of
your folks' shopping bag. Surprisingly though, eggshells also
have a huge amount of strength. You can see this by trying
to break one by squeezing it from top to bottom lengthways
between your thumb and forefinger. Have a try, squeezing it
as hard as you can. Unless there's a structural fault with the
egg (in other words, if it's already cracked) it will be very
difficult, if not impossible, to break.

You can even stand on eggs. This is a brilliant trick to show your mates because no one will believe it works until they see it. And it's dead easy.

Remember – always wash your hands carefully after handling raw eggs to avoid any problems from bacteria.

METHOD

1. Find somewhere to do this – it should be flat and cleanable as you might break the eggs eventually. It's best to do this outside, and definitely NOT on a carpet!

2. Place the tray of eggs on the floor.

3. Bet your mates that you can stand on the eggs without breaking them. At the very least, demand a round of applause if you pull it off.

4. Get one of your friends to stand next to you then put an arm around their shoulder so they take some of your weight. Place one foot flat onto the eggs and put about half of your weight on it, remembering to keep holding onto your friend. Then place the other foot on too. Try to spread your weight evenly between both feet and slowly let go of your friend.

5. Tadaaaa! You are standing on eggs. Applause, please!

6. Now you have a choice. Either wash the eggs and put them away for eating. Or, if you have decided to sacrifice the eggs for the cause of science, give one of your friends a piggyback to see if the eggs will take two of you. Sometimes they will, and sometimes they won't but even so, you should be covered in glory (if not egg yolk)!

GASTROTRUMPS
ANT EGGS

THE STATS

From: Mexico		
Taste: Sweet and milky	7/10	
Smell: None	0/10	
Texture: Creamy little sacs	9/10	
Looks: White jelly beans	8/10	
Adventure level: Cute, but scary	10/10	
Nutritional value: Loads of protein	9/10	
£ Value:	Big treat	

THE LOWDOWN

This Mexican delicacy tastes a bit like caviar (fish eggs) and has a soft shell and a wet runny inside. The creamy taste is an odd but pleasant tongue tickler.

KIT

Large zip-lock plastic bag
Really strong magnet
(preferably a neodymium one)
Packet of cornflakes, rice crispies
or bran flakes (look at the label
and choose a pack with the
highest iron content – usually
14 mg per 100 g)
Rolling pin (optional)

MICROFACT

IF TWO NEODYMIUM MAGNETS SMASH
TOGETHER, THEY CAN SHATTER
DANGEROUSLY.

HOW TO FIND IRON IN YOUR BREAKFAST CEREAL

What!? Are there really lumps of metal in your cereal?
Well, take a peek at the side of the packet. It probably lists a
laboratory-worth of stuff like calcium, vitamin C, magnesium
and iron. These are added to your breakfast so that you grow
up to be the big, strong champion bubble-gum blower you're
capable of being. But if you thought these were all hi-tech
food additives, you'd be wrong. The iron added to your
breakfast is metallic iron, which means that it's basically …
well … bits of iron.

And to prove it to your mates, you can find some in your
cereal using a magnet. Try and get hold of a neodymium
magnet because they're much stronger than normal ceramic
or metal ones like the one in the picture.

METHOD

1. Pour 150 g of cereal onto a clean surface and crush into crumbs
using your hand or a rolling pin.
2. Pour the crumbs into a zip-lock bag and add warm water until it's
¾ full.
3. Carefully seal it, leaving an air gap at the top. Now mix it around
and leave it to soak for 20 minutes or so into a watery mush.
4. Put the magnet on a table and sit the bag on top for about 10
minutes, swilling the contents gently every now and then.
5. VERY carefully lift the bag with one hand, using your other hand to
keep the magnet touching the bag. Where the magnet is touching the
plastic bag, you should be able to see a little smudge of iron. Move the
magnet around a bit and you'll see that there are tiny iron filings following
it around. They're pretty small, but once you spot them, you'll know!

THE STATS

From: South Korea		
Taste: Salty		4/10
Smell: Stale dried fish		2/10
Texture: Wet – it's just tea		5/10
Looks: Like a witch's nightmare		1/10
Adventure level: Evil monster refreshment		8/10
Nutritional value: Not a heck of a lot		1/10
£ Value:		Big treat

THE LOWDOWN

Dried frog skeletons are steeped in hot water to make a medicinal frog-flavoured tea. My friend Yoon Jung says they are mainly bought by parents of kids who try to skive off school saying they're ill. They say, "That's fine, darling – of course you can stay at home. Here's your frog tea." Surprising how few sickies Korean kids pull, isn't it?

ADULT NEEDED

KIT

A handy adult
Knife
Good fat, clean butternut squash,
  carrots, parsnips or other sturdy
  root veg (1 per instrument)
Workbench or clamp
Power drill
Large drill bit (size 14ish)
Smaller drill bit (size 8-9)
Scissors
Thin drinking straws
  (thick ones won't work!)

VEGETABLE INSTRUMENTS

If you've ever been forced by your parents to eat vegetables you didn't like, here's how to get your own back on them (the veg, not your parents). To do this, you need to find yourself a responsible adult (not just any old adult) who's handy with power tools.

Root veg such as carrots, parsnips, turnips and squash make great tootin' flootin' instruments, and with a bit of practise you should be able to make them hoot like a slightly demented musical pig. The noise is perfectly pitched to make grown-ups squeal with pain. Hah!

METHOD

1. Trim the ends off your squash, carrot or parsnip.

2. Secure your vegetable of choice to a workbench (or clamp it to a table) so it doesn't wriggle around.

3. Ask your adult to use the larger drill bit and drill 2/3 into the fattest end of the squash, carrot or parsnip.

4. Ask them to change to the smaller drill bit. They should drill a hole from the other end so that it meets up with the first one. (Depending on the length of your drill bit, you may need to cut the veg down a little.)

5. Now take your vegetable and blow through the small hole to clear out any mushy bits.

6. Using a pair of scissors, cut the drinking straw down to about 12 cm long, then snip the end into a "V" shape and flatten it by squeezing it hard between your fingers. Put the straw into the small drill hole.

7. You're ready to blow. Put the straw about 1 cm into your mouth and blow without biting it. It sometimes takes a bit of fiddling and experimentation to find the right strength of breath and way of blowing, but you should get it. If you really can't get a hoot, try making another instrument.

KIT

A dinner plate with a rim
Milk
3 or 4 different food colourings
Cotton bud
Washing-up liquid

GASTROTRUMPS
SEA SLUG
(OR SEA CUCUMBER)

THE STATS

From: South Korea
Taste: Savoury   6/10
Smell: None   0/10
Texture: Rubbery and crunchy   8/10
Looks: Like a living poo   1/10
Adventure level:
Very cool if you eat this   9/10
Nutritional value:
Mostly water   2/10
£ Value: Pocket money

THE LOWDOWN

These marine gastropod molluscs are found on the sea bed all over the world. Most people leave them right there, but the South Koreans chop the live slug into slices and eat them dipped in soy sauce. The guts taste slightly bitter-sweet.

MILK KALEIDOSCOPE

What have your smelly armpits got in common with plates of slimy chip fat? Oil, my stinky friends.

Now, washing-up liquid, shampoo, soap and shower gel are all basically the same thing. They are emulsifiers, or substances which help water to mix with oil. Normally oil and water don't mix, which is why it's hard to clean greasy plates and armpits. But when an emulsifier like washing-up liquid or soap is added to the water, it mixes with the oil and the combined liquid can then be rinsed away. Bingo! Clean plates and clean pits.

Emulsifiers also do something else that's pretty cool – they weaken surface tension. All liquids have a surface tension and if you very carefully lay a paper clip on the surface of a glass of water, you will see that the surface tension means it stays on the top of the water. Put a drop of washing-up liquid into the water and the emulsifer will weaken the surface tension so that the paper clip will sink to the bottom of the glass.

In this experiment, food colouring is added to the surface of milk and stays in one place. As soon as an emulsifier is added, the colour spreads quickly as the surface tension of milk changes rapidly from the middle outwards.

METHOD

1. Pour milk onto a dinner plate until the base is covered.
2. Very gently put some droplets of the different food colourings around the middle of the milk. The watery colourings should float, but you need to be careful.
3. Put some washing-up liquid on a cotton bud and touch it to the milk in the middle of the plate. Watch as the colour scoots around! Put some more washing-up liquid on the bud and see what happens when you touch the milk in different places.

WHAT HAPPENS WHEN YOU LIQUIDIZE SUNDAY LUNCH?

THE HOTTEST CHILLIES IN THE WORLD

So, one day I thought it might be fun to liquidize Sunday lunch to see what it's like. After all, when you eat food, it all gets mixed together in your stomach and broken down into a big old slurry to help you get all the nutrition out of it. Why not cut out the middleman and just drink your lunch as a sort of smoothie?

To test it out I put a plate of roast beef, roast potatoes, carrots, peas, Brussels sprouts and lashings of gravy into a blender and whizzed the living daylights out of it.

Then I poured the Sunday lunch slurry into a glass. It looked like sloppy poo, which was quite unpleasant. Then I drank it. Ooh. It was nasty and made me want to throw up.

But why? It's just Sunday lunch in another form. Well, the brilliant thing about eating meals with several different foods is that each flavour that our brains sense is usually

(like crunchiness, sliminess, softness or fibrousness). When the taste sensation doesn't match the mouth sensation the brain is expecting, our brains get a little confused and we don't enjoy the food. There you go: I did it so you don't have to!

For reasons that I can never quite remember, my friend Paul thought it would be a good idea to film a scene for one of my TV series where I ate the hottest chillies in the world – something you should never do yourself. As well as being my friend, Paul is a TV executive producer, which sounds grand, but basically

means that he does anything in his power to get people to watch TV programmes, even if it means torturing his mates.

Chillies are wicked. Both wicked-cool and wicked-bad. They're packed with a substance called capsaicin, which stimulates the nerve receptors associated with heat and pain, fooling your nervous system into thinking it's HOT. It's a strange substance because its hotness can't be cooled by water as capsaicin is hydrophobic (it doesn't mix with water, so isn't dissolved by it). The best thing to get rid of a crippling chilli heat is oil, bizarrely, but oil isn't that much fun to drink. The next best cures are milk (because the casein in milk acts like a detergent on it) and a cool sugary drink.

So anyway, the cameras started to roll and in the name of TV I started to eat. First, a red bell pepper. That was fine – it wasn't hot at all. This was going to be easy. Then I ate a jalapeño pepper. YIKES! Hot stuff, but not too bad after the initial shock and a mouthful of milk. Next, a Scotch bonnet. AAAAAWWW! Naaasty. I actually had to jump around to take my mind off the pain. Then a vicious beast: the Naga Jolokia. AAAGHHH! Hyperventilating, breathing gone to pot, a pint of milk. AAAGHHH again! Finally the hottest chilli in the world: the Dorset Naga. It's only a little fella and it doesn't even look particularly nasty.

SHEEEWOOOOOH! My legs started twitching uncontrollably, my heart beat like bad dubstep, while my mind was a nightmarish mix of pain and paranoia. I started running on the spot and swigging milk straight from the bottle. I got through seven litres of milk. Then I fell fast asleep for 30 minutes. From this lesson, we learn one thing: **DON'T EAT RAW CHILLI!**

GASTROTRUMPS
ROTTEN WALRUS
(OR IAUNAK)

THE STATS
From: Arctic Canada
Taste: Rotten liver — 2/10
Smell: Rotten fishy beef — 1/10
Texture: Rotten ham — 1/10
Looks: Rotten dark red meat — 2/10
Adventure level: Gotta get to the Arctic first! — 10/10
Nutritional value: High protein — 9/10
£ Value: Wallet-buster

THE LOWDOWN
This is basically big chunks of walrus, wrapped in plastic and buried underground to rot and freeze. After 12 months, they're dug up and eaten. Try not to vom. It may sound odd, but it's a great way to preserve meat for times of need.

ADULT NEEDED

KIT

A bubbly adult
Safety glasses
2 litre bottle of diet cola –
    at room temperature
Piece of paper
Sticky tape
Pack of Mentos (this will work with
    other types of mint but it won't
    be anywhere near as dramatic)

COLA FOUNTAIN

This is a way of releasing all the carbon dioxide in a bottle of cola, in a very short amount of time. Drop a Mento into the bottle and it turns into a glorious fountain of fizzy drink. Why? Well, the surface of a Mento might look smooth to you, but look really closely – it's actually matt and dull. At microscopic level, Mentos actually have a very rough surface, and the roughness offers the carbon dioxide in the cola little points on which it can turn instantly from dissolved gas into bubbles.

METHOD

1. Be warned – this is going to be messy. Go outside! And wear safety goggles for protection.
2. Stand the cola bottle on some firm ground where it won't fall over and open it carefully.
3. Roll the piece of paper up so that it's just big enough to hold the Mentos and tape it to form a tube. The tube is essential – when the first sweet hits the cola it's going to fizz up pretty quickly so they all need to drop in quickly, smoothly and at the same time.
4. Hold your hand under the bottom of the tube and drop six Mentos into it.
5. Position the tube over the open cola bottle, move your hand away to drop the sweets in and back off quickly.
6. Enjoy the show!

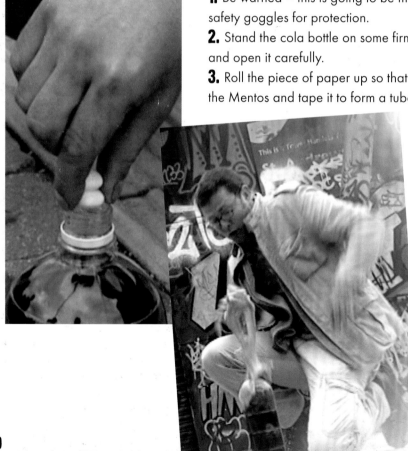

110

BARBECUED SQUIRREL

THE STATS

From: UK

Taste: Meaty and sweet — 8/10

Smell: Smoky, grilled meatiness — 8/10

Texture: Bony little chicken — 8/10

Looks: Teeny-tiny rabbit — 7/10

Adventure level: A bit grim but worthwhile — 9/10

Nutritional value: Excellent lean meat — 8/10

£ Value: Big treat

THE LOWDOWN

Grey squirrels are pests, blamed for spreading diseases that destroy British red squirrels, so eating them is a great way to control their numbers. They are sold at my nearest big supermarket in North London every now and then, and they make an unusual addition to the BBQ. Wrap them in streaky bacon first as they don't have much fat on them and would otherwise dry out.

KIT

A cheeky adult
Knife
Blender or food processor
Small red cabbage
Sieve
Big bowl
4 small glasses or bottles
1 tsp washing powder
1 tsp vinegar
½ tsp baking powder

CABBAGE COLOUR CHEMISTRY

If you don't like cabbage, it's probably down to the sulphurous flavours that are releaseed when it's cooked. The more it's cooked, the more powerful those flavour compounds become, so overcooked cabbage is definitely more ... cabbagey. Some of these sugars are relatively indigestible and are dealt with in your large intestine by fart-producing bacteria. (This may make you enjoy cabbage more – it certainly works for me.) If you do like the taste of cabbage, I salute you. If you still don't, stop eating it and try this little experiment. You can use the secret chemicals in red cabbage to tell whether something is acid or alkaline. It's bloomin' good stuff.

WHAT'S REALLY HAPPENING

Red cabbage and purple carrots contain amazing secret chemicals called anthocyanins. These are very sensitive molecules which change colour depending on how acidic their environment is, for example if they are mixed with an acid (a low-pH substance like lemon juice) or an alkali (high-pH like washing powder). Diluted red cabbage juice is neither acidic nor alkali so it's pH neutral and looks bluey-purple. Add some lemon juice and it changes colour to pinky-red. Add washing powder and it will turn green. Pretty cool stuff.

METHOD

1. With an adult to help you, chop half a small red cabbage into large chunks and put it in the blender or food processor. Add a glass or two of water and blend it for several minutes until you're left with a pulpy mush.

2. Place a sieve over a bowl (to catch the purpley cabbage liquid) and pour the pulp into it. Squish it down to get as much liquid out as possible. Pour some plain water into four glasses and put them on a table that's OK to get messy. Add a tablespoon of cabbage water to each glass so that they turn bright blue.

3. Add a spoonful of washing powder to one glass and stir it well. It should turn green. (This sounds weird, but it goes green because it's an alkaline chemical.)

4. Add a spoonful of vinegar to another glass and watch it turn red. (This is because vinegar is an acid.)

5. Add half a spoonful of baking powder to another glass and watch it turn into a fizzing, frothing glass of bubbles. (This is less to do with acidity or alkalinity, but it is great fun!)

6. Keep the last glass blue to remember what it looks like!

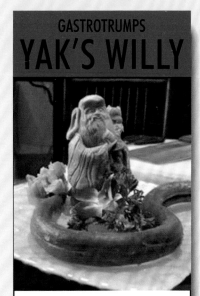

GASTROTRUMPS
YAK'S WILLY

THE STATS

From: China

Taste: Porky		6/10
Smell: Clean, meaty		4/10
Texture: Crunchy		6/10
Looks: Yak's unmentionables		6/10
Adventure level: Only the very brave		10/10
Nutritional value: Good lean protein		8/10
£ Value:		Wallet-buster

THE LOWDOWN

The Chinese are brilliant at eating every edible part of an animal and wasting nothing. You'd have thought they might stop at willies, but no! I went to a restaurant in Beijing that specializes in them and was served a plate of assorted willies including deer, pig, yak, bull and goat. Brings tears to a boy's eyes!

WHY DO ONIONS MAKE YOU CRY?

used to think I was pretty tough but the truth is, I'm not. To be more specific, I have very sensitive eyes. I once made a TV series in which I visited people living in difficult or dangerous conditions, and I would always find myself hunched over an open fire in a tiny mud hut or cooking squirrel in a jungle. The smoke from these fires would get in my eyes and I would be crying within seconds, while trying to interview someone for the camera. I spent the entire series looking like an emotional and physical wreck!

I get the same problem with onions. Even chopping up a spring onion can turn on the waterworks, let alone powerful medium-sized onions. Most people have a teary-eyed reaction to cutting raw onions, and here's why.

When you cut a raw onion you break open its microscopic cells which contain loads of interesting sulphur compounds as well as chemicals called enzymes. These quickly react with other chemicals in the onion to create sulphenic acids which further react to create a gas called syn-propanethial-S-oxide. This is also known as onion lachrymatory factor synthase (lachrymatory means "causing tears"), which is an eye irritant. Your tear glands produce tears to flush the irritant away, and Bob's your teary uncle.

There are loads of old wives tales about how to stop onions making you cry, and I've tried them all: wearing glasses, chilling the onions. I've even been seen in the kitchen wearing a snorkel and mask. NONE of them stopped me crying, because the irritant can find its way towards your eyes even if you just breathe it in.

The only thing that really seems to work is to cut the onions under water. The downside is that if you cut onions under water, you could slice your finger – don't do it!

COOKING WITH LIQUID NITROGEN

Liquid nitrogen is super-chilly: -196°C. It's so cold that if you dunk a flower in it and then squeeze it, it shatters. So, on one level, liquid nitrogen is a heck of a lot of fun, but on another level, it's extremely dangerous.

You can't carry liquid nitrogen around in a closed container because it creates so much pressure as it warms up (as it changes from a liquid to a gas, it expands by over 1000 times) that it could blow up the container. So you have to carry it in open Dewar flasks, which allow the gas to escape through the lid. Nitrogen isn't dangerous for us – every breath we take

is 78% nitrogen, but when you have too much of any gas in a room, it can force out all the oxygen, which we DO need (it's called "displacement"). This is why you aren't allowed to take it in a lift: if the lift got stuck, the nitrogen would slowly leak from the Dewar and force out all the other gases including oxygen, and you'd suffocate. Oh, happy days.

On the plus side, liquid nitrogen is actually pretty cheap at about 20p a litre. After all, it's distilled from the cheapest substance on earth – air – in an amazing process called fractional distillation. Air is collected, cooled to incredibly low temperatures and pressurized until it becomes liquid air. Then it's slowly warmed up and the different

gases boil off. When it hits -196°C the nitrogen boils off and can be collected.

Why am I telling you all this? Because liquid nitrogen is used a lot in food processing – it's perfectly safe to consume, so it can be added to food to rapidly cool it. For instance, after mayonnaise has been heated, liquid nitrogen can be used to cool it quickly before it's packaged. My crazy chemistry professor friend Dr Sella (Clever Fella) and I often use it to make ice cream super quickly. And the quicker you make it, the smoother it is. He can also use it to turn himself into a dragon, but that's so dangerous I'm not allowed to tell you how he does it!

KIT
A jar (or a lunchbox) with an airtight lid

GASTROTRUMPS
DUCK GUTS

THE STATS
From: Mexico
Taste: Like petroly offal   4/10
Smell: Smoky   6/10
Texture: Stringy and chewy   3/10
Looks: Worms   1/10
Adventure level:
Pretty cool   8/10
Nutritional value:
Fat and protein   5/10
£ Value: Big treat

THE LOWDOWN
Duck intestines are a delicacy in Mexico but are pretty rare, even in Mexico City. They are cleaned then smoked and eaten either as an ingredient in a stew or as a little snack.

HOW TO CATCH FARTS IN A JAR

I've always thought that the world would be a better place if we all kept our farts in jars. I'm sure you've always wondered how Napoleon's were flavoured, how badly Shakespeare whiffed, or whether or not Christopher Columbus was a stinker.

So let's get the farty ball rolling now, my friends and the generations who follow us can be enlightened by our captured gas. Here's how to do it.

METHOD
1. Eat the World's Fartiest Meal (p. 64), then wait until you've brewed up a great head of steam. When you're up to flatulent speed, run yourself a bath.

2. Get in the bath. I should point out that baths are traditionally taken with no clothes on, but I'll leave that up to you.

3. Hop out of the bath and grab your jar – sorry, I should have said that earlier. Now get back in. Won't happen again.

4. Take the lid off the jar and keep it handy. Submerge the jar so that it's full of water and, under the surface, turn it upside down, so that the opening of the jar is facing downwards.

5. Position the jar above your bum and squeeze out a fart so that when it rises, it gets trapped in the jar. This is called water displacement, and was famously discovered by Archimedes around 250 BC with a shriek of "Eureka!". If your folks complain that I'm just teaching you how to be rude, you can tell them the sciencey bits.

6. Keep going until your jar is as full as possible then, keeping the jar upside down, put the lid on UNDER THE WATER. There will still be water in the jar, but that's fine. Turn it the right way up and hop out.

7. Share your captured farts as you see fit, or save them for posterity.

ADULT NEEDED

KIT

A relatively responsible adult
500 g large potatoes
Peeler
Knife
370 ml water
Blender or food processor
Clean tea towel
Sieve
Large saucepan
Wooden spoon
2 tsp vinegar
2 tsp liquid glycerine (you'll
  find this in supermarket
  baking section)
5 drops food colouring
  (any colour)
2 baking trays
Foil
Vegetable oil
Staples and sellotape

MICROFACT

HAMBURGERS ARE NOT MADE OF HAM.
IS IT ONLY ME WHO THINKS THAT
CALLING A BEEFBURGER AFTER A PORK
PRODUCT IS WEIRD? THE NAME COMES
FROM THE GERMAN PORT OF HAMBURG
AND HAS ONLY BEEN AROUND SINCE
1890, UNLIKE "PIZZA" WHICH HAS
BEEN USED SINCE AD 997.

HOW TO MAKE A PLASTIC BAG OUT OF POTATOES

Recycle this, compost that! People are always trying to make you feel guilty about stuff, but often they don't go far enough. Make this wildly biodegradeable plastic bag out of potatoes and send them off to the shops with it!

METHOD

1. Peel the potatoes then chop them into small cubes.

2. Put half of the raw potato chunks in the blender with 125 ml of the water and get an adult to help you blend them on full power for 2 minutes until you've got a smooth pulp.

3. Place the clean tea towel in the sieve and pour the potato pulp into it to drain. Blend the other batch of potatoes and water and add them to the sieve.

4. Gently squeeze the pulp to get rid of some more water, then leave it for 10 minutes to drain.

5. Pour 120 ml cold water into a large saucepan, add 20 g of your potato pulp, two teaspoons of vinegar, two teaspoons of glycerine and five drops of food colouring.

6. With your grown-up's help, put the saucepan on a low heat and stir with a wooden spoon constantly as it warms up. When it begins to thicken, turn the heat up and keep stirring until it boils. Keep it boiling for 5 minutes, stirring very carefully, and then turn the heat off.

7. Cover both baking trays with foil and lightly oil them using a splash of vegetable oil. Put your oven on low (about 65°C/gas 1).

8. Spread the mixture over the trays to make two large sheets – these will be the sides of the bag, so make them as flat, neat and wide as you can, without leaving any holes. Put them in the oven for 2 hours to dry (alternatively leave them in a warm room for 24 hours).

9. When they are completely dry, cut them into equal shapes, cut a neat handle-hole in the top and staple them together. Strengthen the joins with sellotape and you're away!

ADULT NEEDED

KIT

An adult

Safety glasses

Empty film canisters (one is fine, but 10 would be 10 times cooler)

Few pieces of loo roll (tissues don't work, strangely)

Lemon juice (easiest to buy in bottles from a shop, but you can always squeeze your own lemons)

1 tsp bicarbonate of soda (NOT baking soda) for each rocket

FOOD-POWERED MINI ROCKETS

I LOVE blowing things up – preferably with food. Obviously, it's only in the pursuit of knowledge ... ahem, or science ... or something.

There are a couple of ways to make food-powered rockets, and they all involve some element of danger, so you MUST have an adult to help, and you must do this outside.

These are really simple little mini rockets powered by a cake ingredient. When you mix bicarbonate of soda and an acidic liquid like lemon juice or vinegar, a reaction happens which gives off loads of carbon dioxide, building up the pressure in a container that is released by the lid blowing off! A good one will fly about five metres into the air.

You need to get hold of some all-white plastic film canisters (the grey-lidded ones won't work), which is easy – just drop into a photo developing shop and ask very nicely if they've got any spare. They aren't much use to anyone so they might even give them to you for free.

METHOD

1. Make sure you have a handy adult and a pair of safety glasses – it's going to get explosive!

2. Pour 2 tbsp of lemon juice into each film canister.

3. Lay a sheet of loo roll over the top of each canister and press down a little to make a small dip. (This will keep the liquid and powder apart until ready.)

4. Put a teaspoon of baking soda in each little dip of the loo roll.

5. Gently but firmly push the lids onto the pots, so that the baking powder is sitting just below the lid.

6. Carefully take the pots outside and find a clear place that's OK to get messy.

7. Turn the pots upside down and stand well back.

8. In about 5–30 seconds they should pop into the air. If one doesn't (occasionally there's a glitch), wait at least 3 minutes before picking it up (I don't want it going off in your face). Then, holding it pointing away from you, pop the lid off.

9. Now clear up the mess before you get into trouble!

BAMBOO GRUBS

THE STATS

From: Burma
Taste: Sweet, Jerusalem artichoke-y   **8/10**
Smell: Musky   **5/10**
Texture: Crispy   **7/10**
Looks: Maggots   **1/10**
Adventure level:
Weirdy-beardy   **8/10**
Nutritional value:
High protein, low fat   **9/10**
£ Value: **Big treat**

THE LOWDOWN

The Karen people in Eastern Burma are desperately poor but extraordinarily kind, and they served me these grubs that are found in bamboo stalks as a huge treat. The live grubs are simply dry-fried in a pan and they taste wonderfully sweet, but bizarrely similar to raw Jerusalem artichokes.

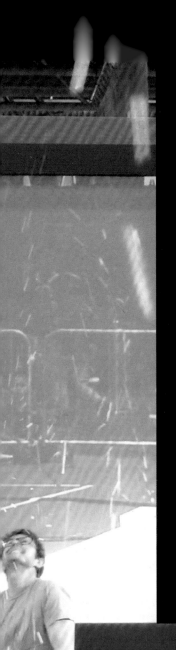

KIT

Large plastic or
  heatproof bowl
Smaller plastic or
  heatproof bowl
Water – you can use tap water,
  although distilled water (from
  hardware shops) tends to make
  clearer ice
Flowers, toys or sweets
Something heavy e.g. cans
  of food

HOW TO MAKE AN ICE BOWL

This is wicked: it's spectacular and it's free because it's just made of water. It does need to freeze overnight, though, so you'll need to start it the day before you want it. You can even make it days or weeks in advance and store it in the freezer.

Basically, you fill up one bowl with water, then push another bowl down into it to make the water between the two bowls turn into a bowl-shape, then it's frozen solid. Use your ice bowl at a party to serve ice cream or fruit in, or to keep your drinks cold.

METHOD

1. Make sure your large bowl can fit in the available space in your freezer. (The bigger the bowl, the more spectacular it will be, but it needs to fit inside!)

2. Line the bowl with some fun fillings – flowers, toys or sweets.

3. Put the bowl in the sink (to catch spillages) and fill it about 2/3 of the way up with water.

4. Push the smaller bowl down into the water until it sits on top of the fillings. Then weigh it down with something heavy, such as cans of food.

5. CAREFULLY put the whole thing into the freezer and leave to set for 12–24 hours until frozen solid.

6. When the bowl has set, take it out of the freezer. To remove the moulds, fill your sink about 10 cm full of warm water and put the frozen bowls into it. Remove the weights and then fill the middle bowl with warm water to help release it. After a few minutes you should be able to gently lift it out. Next, slowly ease the ice bowl out of the large bowl. You may need to help it along by adding some extra

MICROFACT

HUMANS CAN'T DIGEST GRASS UNLIKE
COWS, WHO HAVE AN EXTRA BIT OF GUT
CALLED A RUMEN TO DEAL WITH IT.
EVEN THOUGH WE CAN'T BREAK DOWN
THE CELLULOSE IN GRASS, IT'S STILL
POSSIBLE TO EAT. IN FACT, WE NEED
INDIGESTIBLE MATTER (ROUGHAGE) TO
KEEP OUR GUT HEALTHY.

warm water to the sink. Once it's out of the mould, you can put the bowl back in the freezer where it will keep for months.

7. When you're ready to use it, remember to put it onto a tray as it will slowly melt in the warmth.

GASTROTRUMPS
DUCK HEADS

THE STATS

From: China
Taste: Salty, sweet, meaty   7/10
Smell: Smoky, treacly   7/10
Texture: Fatty, bony   2/10
Looks: Dead duck   4/10
Adventure level:
Need to be pretty brave   9/10
Nutritional value:
Not a heck of a lot on
them, to be honest   2/10
£ Value: Pocket money

THE LOWDOWN
Duck heads are a bit like pig
trotters and chicken feet – you
gnaw at them and they taste
lovely as they're usually cooked
in soy sauce and sugar. Duck
heads have an added bonus –
you can crack them open and
spoon out the brains. Great stuff!

CAN YOU EAT FOOD FLAVOURED WITH PERFUME?

Perfume companies spend millions of pounds coming up with the most glamorous and exotic flavours on earth, so I've always wondered why they don't use those amazing flavours in food. Wouldn't it make sense to sell us perfume-flavoured crisps, aftershave chocolate or ketchup *eau de toilette*? These people are missing a trick!

While these meanies deny us the delights of perfumed food, I thought I'd try it out myself. So I stirred cologne into my scrambled eggs, added aftershave to my gravy and drizzled perfume onto my chips. Then I sat down for lunch. VOMORAMA! It was absolutely disgusting!

Those flavours weren't built for food. My eggs tasted like estate agent in cheap suit, my gravy smelt like old granny, and my chips had such a bitter tang that they were impossible to keep down. The trouble with these flavours is that they aren't ones that we normally associate with food, so our brains are confused when we mix them. And the taste (the part of it that we sense on our tongues) is ruined by the strange alcohols in the perfume, which is where the bitterness comes from. That's why we don't use perfume as a flavour. So don't bother trying.

FLAME-THROWER-GRILLED MARSHMALLOWS

This is one of the most ridiculous things I've ever done, but it was so much fun I've got to tell you about it. One day I took five young mates to a company

MICROFACT

PARENTS HATE E NUMBERS SO THEY PREFER YOUR SWEETS TO BE COLOURED WITH THINGS LIKE NATURAL BEETROOT EXTRACT. WHAT THEY DON'T KNOW IS THAT NATURAL BEETROOT EXTRACT IS ALSO KNOWN AS E162.

which creates special effects for big movies. They built us a special massive flame-thrower for us so that we could grill marshmallows in an instant. We all had a great time blasting the living daylights out of various foods: caramelizing a crème caramel, browning a lasagne, grilling some delicious marshmallows and incinerating toast. It works – but as a cooking technique it's a little ...

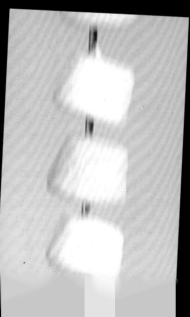

KIT

An adult
A knife
3 x 2p pieces
3 zinc nails (from a
  hardware shop)
3 large baking potatoes
Small battery-powered alarm
  clock
4 x 10 cm pieces of
  electrical wire
8 small crocodile clips (from an
  electronics shop) – sticky tape
  would just about do, although
  it'll be a bit fiddly!

ELECTRIC POTATOES

You can get an electric current from some amazing substances – lemons are pretty easy, and I've managed to power a clock from potatoes and even cheese sandwiches. Basically, this technique is about moving electrons from a copper coin to a zinc nail, using the medium of the food they're stuck into! And that flow of electrons can power a small electronic device.

METHOD

1. Ask an adult to help you cut one small slit in each potato – big enough to jam the coin in so that it doesn't slip out.

2. Push a coin into each slit, then 3 cm away from the coin push a zinc nail halfway down. Do this to each potato.

3. Remove the battery from the clock, and clip (or stick) one end of a piece of wire to the negative (–) terminal of the battery casing in the clock and clip the other end to the coin in the potato.

4. Clip another piece of wire from the nail in potato one and join the other end to the coin in potato two.

5. Clip another piece of wire from the nail in potato two to the coin in potato three.

6. Clip another piece of wire from the nail in potato three to the positive (+) terminal in the alarm clock. The clock should turn on and start to work. If there's any problem, check all the connections and if your potatoes really don't work, try lemons instead!

MICROFACT

A FRENCHMAN ONCE ATE AN AEROPLANE, A BICYCLE AND A TV. MICHEL LOTITO DRANK MINERAL OIL TO WASH DOWN INDIGESTIBLE OBJECTS TO ENTERTAIN PEOPLE. THE CESSNA 150 AEROPLANE TOOK ABOUT 2 YEARS TO SCOFF.

ACKNOWLEDGEMENTS

I would like to thank the glorious BBC, brilliant crews, fantastic kids, generous teachers, Denise Johnstone-Burt, Nic Knight, Louise Jackson, Charlie Moyler, Paul Gilheany, Damian Kavanagh, Anne Gilchrist, Atul Malhotra, Bridget Banton, Alison Gregory, Borra Garson, Jan Croxson, Kate Mander, Andrea Sella (Clever Fella) and the delicious Georgia, Daisy and Poppy...
I've been having more fun than I ever believed possible making *Gastronuts* and *Incredible Edibles*. Thank you, thank you, thank you all from the bottom of my heart.

The ingredients, nutritional value and/or statements in any recipes included in this book are not intended as medical advice. All recipes are for informational, educational, and/or entertainment purposes only. If in doubt, please consult a health professional.

The publishers are not held responsible for any damage, injury or loss resulting from failure to correctly follow any instructions in this book.

First published 2012 by Walker Books Ltd, 87 Vauxhall Walk, London SE11 5HJ

2 4 6 8 10 9 7 5 3 1

Text © 2012 Stefan Gates
Photographs © 2012 Georgia Glynn Smith
Stills from "Gastronuts" and "Incredible Edibles" © 2012 Objective Productions Ltd
Surströmming photograph (p.63) © 2006 Erik Forsberg
Cane Rat photograph (p.91) © 2008 UENP
Naked Egg photograph (p.97) © 2011 Amy Snyder/ Exploratorium

The publishers would like to thank Erik Forsberg for permission to use his photograph of surströmming, the UENP for permission to use their photograph of a cane rat, the Exploratorium (www.exploratorium.edu) for permission to use their photograph of a naked egg and Bompass and Parr for the jelly mould on p. 57.

The right of Stefan Gates to be identified as the author of this work has been asserted by him in accordance with the Copyright, Designs and Patents Act 1988.

This book has been typeset in Futura Printed in Belgium

British Library Cataloguing in Publication Data: a catalogue record for this book is available from the British Library.

ISBN 978-1-4063-3906-2

www.thegastronaut.com
www.walker.co.uk